What Is "Real Believing"?

Lewis B. Smedes explains it as "the kind you do with your deepest self, down where your primeval feelings flow. It's a feeling that lets you know in the deepest places of your soul it is all right even when your head tells you everything is ghastly."

"Smedes explores in successive chapters God's various gifts: grace, joy, forgiveness, etc. Extremely honest, with a wry, slightly ironical style that cuts through clichés."

—*Library Journal*

"Smedes's casual, colloquial style proves to be a surprisingly good vehicle for some very serious business . . . unusual candor and realism."

—*Kirkus Reviews*

Books by Lewis B. Smedes

Forgive and Forget
How Can It Be All Right When
  Everything Is All Wrong?

Published by POCKET BOOKS

Most Pocket Books are available at special quantity discounts for bulk purchases for sales promotions, premiums or fund raising. Special books or book excerpts can also be created to fit specific needs.

For details write the office of the Vice President of Special Markets, Pocket Books, 1230 Avenue of the Americas, New York, New York 10020.

How Can It Be All Right When Everything Is All Wrong?

Lewis B. Smedes

PUBLISHED BY POCKET BOOKS NEW YORK

POCKET BOOKS, a division of Simon & Schuster, Inc.
1230 Avenue of the Americas, New York, N.Y. 10020

Published by arrangement with Harper & Row Publishers, Inc.
Library of Congress Catalog Card Number: 82-47756

ISBN: 0-671-60712-X

First Pocket Books printing September, 1986

10 9 8 7 6 5 4 3 2 1

POCKET and colophon are registered trademarks
of Simon & Schuster, Inc.

Printed in the U.S.A.

To Joan
    And to Leslie, Sara,
    Dirk, and Paul

Contents

Invitation

If you are trying hard to believe in God while a hundred voices inside tell you to stop believing, you are my kind of person. I wrote this book for you.

Believing does not come easy for me either. It never has come easy; I suppose it never will. I almost always believe in God in spite of problems and pains that tell me things are so wrong that believing in a good God doesn't make sense. The things I say here are filtered through many years of believing against the grain.

Too many people I care about hurt too much to let believing come easy. People close to me get cancer and die too soon; my prayers do not take away the pain or hold back the tolling of the bells. My friends' marriages turn into battlefields and their children go through a hundred kinds of mini-hells. God does not do many miracles for my crowd.

But the pains of people in my little orbit are just starters. Those starving children I pray for across the sea keep on dying; and the oppressed people I pray for keep getting their heads banged and their freedoms choked. I am not whimpering. I know we make many of our own miseries. I am only admitting that, when I believe that God really cares, I feel a lot of hurts that tell me he does not seem to care enough.

Faith does not break loose in my head with a whooping, "Hurrah for God!" Believing sneaks into my soul while my mind is saying, "My God, where were you when I needed you?"

I am talking about real believing, the kind you do with your deepest self, down where your primeval feelings flow. The thinking part is not all that hard. I can think of arguments for God in my sleep. It is the feeling part that comes hard, the part that lets you know in the deep places of your soul that it is all right even when your head tells you everything is ghastly.

Deep feeling, fiercer than mere emotion, is what I have in mind. I am talking about the feelings that grab you at the core of your being and tell you whether life is good or rotten. These are the feelings that push your life toward joy or misery. We are talking about feelings of the heart, the window of your being where you are open to God.

When I *feel* that I am loved while everything about me says I am unlovable, then I am believing, really believing. When I *feel* that life in this valley of death is much worth the living, then I am believing. When I *feel* gratitude enough to make me glad, then I am believing. When I *feel* that all is right with me even when everything around me is the pits, then I am actually believing.

The feeling takes hold of us in many levels of our living. In this book I invite you to look around on a dozen different levels of your life to see whether you have discovered a sense of all-rightness there, in your own feelings. Each chapter is a story of discovery, a disclosure that it can be all right when things are brutally bad.

Discovery, I say! Not achievement. We are not talking about "trying harder." If you have the feeling yourself—the primitive intuition that comes deep beneath the surface of brain-waves—you will know it is a gift. A gift of grace? Of course, what else? Good old amazing grace, it is still the bottom line of discovery.

I do not want to mislead you. I have no bag of religious tricks to make everything turn out well for you. This is not a spiritual "how-to" sort of book. I do not know how to stage-manage grace. I do not know how to command grace when to appear and how to make its entrance. I think it fiercely sinful to try. I only know how to recognize the gifts of grace when I see them, strangely and freely given. And what I offer in this book are some hints as to where you can see them. And feel them.

Grace does come, this I know for sure.

Grace happens to me when I feel a surge of honest joy that makes me glad to be alive in spite of valid reasons for feeling terrible. Grace happens when I accept my wife's offer to begin again with me in love after I have hurt her. It happens when I feel powerfully free to follow my own conscience in spite of those who think I am either crazy or wicked. Grace is the gift of feeling sure that our future, even our dying, is going to turn out more splendidly than we dare imagine. Grace is the feeling of hope.

Yes, grace does happen. It happens on many

11

layers of my life. But one thing is the same all the way through. Grace makes me feel that it's all right even when everything is all wrong.

If you, like me, are a believer in spite of yourself, you may see yourself in some of the discoveries of grace in this book. If you come along, I hope you will remember great moments when you too were simply seized by a joy of feeling that all was right with you. I hope even more that it will happen again, maybe while you read. If it does, let the flames of feeling burn until you know in your heart that all is right with you again.

How Can It Be All Right When Everything Is All Wrong?

1. When Everything Is Really Bad, There's Only One Word for It

◈§ THE GIFT OF GRACE §◈

Grace be with you.
Col. 4:18b, RSV

I walked away from Cal's hospital bed, opened the door, and stopped for a moment to look back before I left him. He lifted his head a bit, smiled, and said, "It's all right." And then I left him, and never saw him again. But his words have haunted me ever since, and have become for me a metaphor of life's deepest question. How can anyone really believe that it is all right when everything is hopelessly wrong?

When I heard that my best friend was dying of cancer, I flew to Michigan from Los Angeles to spend a few days with him while he still had strength to talk. Cal and I had been friends since we met on the first day of our first year of college. I knew this would be the last time we would talk on earth, after thirty years of a friendship that has never been replaced. We spent four days talking together about our past and about his future, as only deeply good friends can talk. And then I had to leave. Three days later he would be dead. But as I

15

looked over my shoulder to be in touch with his eyes for one last living moment, he left me the haunting heritage of those commonplace words: "It's all right."

When I left his room and walked toward the elevator, his wife, Joan, grabbed me and cried, "Lew, I'm scared." And I knew that it was not all right. It was all wrong. It was all wrong for his wife. It was all wrong for his four children. It was all wrong for his friends. As I rode down the elevator toward the hospital lobby, I cried my pitiful complaints to God that it was all wrong for me. By the time I got to my car, I knew that I was going to be put through the wringer of this terrible question for a long time to come. How can we be ground down in pain and grief and death and still believe that it's all right at the center of life? The answer must be blowing somewhere in the winds of grace.

Have you ever noticed how commonplaces come alive as uncommon truth when they come at just the right time? What a trite comfort: "It's all right." A boy strikes out in a Little League game: "It's all right," says his coach. A guest spills coffee on a clean tablecloth: "It's all right," says the hostess. A baby cries in the night: "It's all right," says the mother. Clichés of reassurance about things a lot less than life or death. But now my friend was not talking about spilled coffee or a missed pitch; he was talking about life at its depths. In this setting, the commonplace becomes either profound self-deception or uncommon truth.

The word "grace" has often been no more than a commonplace pleasantry. St. Paul picked up the old bromide from a trivial custom of his time, and closed all of his letters with a variation on the "grace" theme: "Grace be with you," he said, or something similar. What a cliché! You could have heard it everywhere Greek was spoken in those days. A man lifted a glass of wine to a stranger he met at a bar and said, "Here's grace to you." He signed off a letter to a person he despised, "Grace be with you." A stale, flip, silly little lie people used to oil the machinery of trivial conversation. A commonplace, nothing more.

But now St. Paul rescued this anemic commonplace, dipped it into a whole new reality, and made it a signal of God's assurance that *life can be all right just when everything in it is all wrong.* The reality of Jesus transformed the cliché of grace into the reality of God, coming into our time, our history, our lives, to make things right at the center. He came as a living person called Jesus, talking and hurting and dying, and coming to life again; his mission was to bring grace to the world, and so in deepest reality to make it All Right precisely when things are all wrong. Grace? It is shorthand for everything that God is and does for us in our tired and sinful broken lives. Grace be to you! It's all right even though it's all wrong. Commonplace? No more.

We are picking up a hint even now about how grace works. Grace does not make everything right. Grace's trick is to show us that it is right for us to live; that it is truly good, wonderful even, for us to be breathing and feeling at the same time that everything clustering around us is wholly wretched. Grace is not a ticket to Fantasy Island; Fantasy Island is dreamy fiction. Grace is not a potion to charm life to our liking; charms are magic. Grace does not cure all our cancers, transform all our kids into winners, or send us all soaring into the high skies of sex and success. Grace is rather an amazing power to look earthy reality full in the face, see its sad and tragic edges, feel its cruel cuts, join in the primeval chorus against its outrageous unfairness, and yet feel in your deepest being that it is good and right for you to be alive on God's good earth. Grace is power, I say, to see life very clearly, admit it is sometimes all wrong, and still know that somehow, in the center of your life, "It's all right." This is one reason we call it amazing grace.

Grace is the one word for all that God is for us in the form of Jesus Christ. But it has many faces. I will focus here on three faces of grace, three profiles of God's amazing way of getting to us when we are down: grace is pardon; grace is power; grace is promise. I invite you to look at each of them with me. As we talk of them, please remember that grace is not an idea, but a reality; and you know it not when you say the words, but when God gives you the gift.

GRACE IS PARDON

The bedrock of grace is the amazing gift of knowing that it is all right with us personally when we know that a lot of things are wrong with us.

Do any of our lives match our early dreams? Do our characters live up to the fine visions that filtered through our fantasies in brighter, more innocent days? Once, when we still dreamed dreams, we thought we had a chance at that elusive blend, that ideal mix, happiness and goodness; we would be both rich *and* generous, sexy *and* virtuous. We believed we might actually become that creative, credible, and complete person we knew we really had it in us to be. But, God help us, look at us now.

If we do not match our own dreams, what about the dreams God has for us? God's dream for human life came true in Jesus Christ. He is the profile of God's sort of person. Forget now about his eternal deity; concentrate on the human person—working with fierce honesty through a hypocritical culture, with fine compassion through a heartless religious system, risking everything that ordinary people want out of life so he could minister to lost and hurt human beings, freely led by sacrificial love into the most untimely death in human history. What a person! And he is God's image for us. The word is: be like Jesus if you want to be God's kind of human being.

But what can we do when we have not come close to letting God's dream of goodness come true in us? Is religion our refuge? Let me warn you. A religion without grace will wallop you with God's image of the perfect human life; it will condemn you for not matching it in your own life. Religion clobbers you for your failures, and sends you groveling in the sawdust of defeat. I spoke with a middle-aged woman recently who had just come hurting and shamed through a divorce and felt condemned by a religion without grace; she said to me, "I know that I will never be able to forgive myself." What? Never? Never forgive yourself? Never smile again and say, "It's all right even though I may have been all wrong"? Religion sometimes does this to us; it tells us that we're forever wrong unless we measure up to God's ideal.

Grace to you, dear woman, and grace to all of us when we fall short of God's perfect image of human life! May grace break through to you in your real and in your false guilt, your serious guilt and your petty guilt. May grace come to convince you at the depths of your soul that it's all right even though a lot is wrong with you. It will happen to you, you will know it, feel it, live it, when God persuades you that, as far as he is concerned, in spite of everything, all is right with you.

This is one amazing thing about grace, its surprising contradiction of the tender conscience. Conscience condemns; grace contradicts its condemnation. Conscience says, It's all wrong because you are wrong. Grace says, It's all right even if you are wrong. Grace is always a surprise. It is not surprising that God wants us to be good; it is not surprising that God wants us to be honest, fair, decent, and kind. Every deity conceived in the pious imaginations of religious folk wants these things. But the surprising word of the amazing God of Jesus Christ, the word coming from the cross where he died to make it right, the good word to a sinful soul, is this word: it is all right, at the very core of life, all right, precisely when we are in the wrong. This is pardon, the first face of the grace that embraces us.

GRACE IS POWER

Grace, in its second face, is the power to lead you closer to his image and make you a better person today than you were yesterday. But we will not sense how amazing this power is unless we see that it is unlike any energy we manipulate through our technology. Grace is a power totally unlike any we create in nuclear reactors; it is different from all physical force. But it is different, too, from moral force; grace does not make us better people by bullying us into moral improvement. The power to make us better works when God freely persuades us that it is all right with us the way we are. The power of grace is paradoxical.

When you are freed by pardoning grace, you are most powerful. When you feel sure that you can never be condemned for what you are, that no judgment, no catastrophic guilt can hurt you, the power begins to work! When grace persuades you it is all right with you even when you are wrong, then the power begins to work to make you right.

Don Quixote, that ridiculous knight who came riding on his silly donkey to conquer his crazy world, is a splendid secular parable of amazing grace. Quixote ended up tilting at windmills, but he had one powerful ability. He was able to make life better for someone by persuading her it was all right when things were really all wrong. He met this tawdry woman in a tawdry tavern in a tawdry little town. She was not a fine woman; in fact, everyone in town knew she was a bad woman. Since they all knew she was bad, they all treated her like a hopelessly dirty sinner. And, since everyone treated her like a bad woman, she felt she must *be* a bad woman. So she acted the part. Then the amazing Don Quixote rode into town. He looked at her through the spectacles of his grace. What he saw was a splendid woman. He broke through the icy judgment of the moral majority and declared her to be a fine and noble person. He said to her: "It's all right even though everyone says you're all wrong." And when she was sure that Don Quixote really meant it, when she embraced the grace with which he embraced her, she began to *feel* the *power* of grace. She became what Don Quixote saw.

But now back to the reality of God's grace. We are not dealing with a fictional knight who jousts with windmill blades. We are dealing with a holy and an honest God who expects us to be holy and knows we are not. But God works with us, too, on the premise that we are all right when we know a lot is wrong with us. Consider two examples. Peter denied Jesus, to save face in front of a chambermaid, said he never knew the man, and when he faced up to his cowardliness he cried, "I am a Christ-denier!" (Luke 22:54–62).* At the moment he confessed, he heard God say, "It's all right, even now, when you are so terribly wrong." At *that* moment, the moment of his most contemptible weakness, when he embraced the grace that embraced him, he received power to be an apostle of Christ instead of a denier of Christ.

St. Paul was an apostle-killer. He had a moral monster on his conscience, and when he confronted it, he saw himself as all wrong: "I'm the kind of person who kills apostles" (Acts 26:9–11). But when he acknowledged his horrible identity crisis, he also heard God say: "It's all right even when you

---

*Bible quotations are in the author's own paraphrase, unless otherwise noted.

22

are awesomely wrong" (Acts 26:12–18). And that was when he felt power to become, instead of an apostle-killer, the greatest of all apostles.

And so it goes. The moment we know it's all right even though we are grotesquely in the wrong, we are liberated from our private burden of failures and given power to become the sort of person God wants us to be. To put it theologically, the moment we feel our justification, we are on the way to sanctification. The straitjacket of self-hatred is off; the shackles of self-judgment are ripped away; the liberating power is set loose, and we are on the way to becoming the person we are meant to be. This surprising power of grace is the second face of grace.

GRACE IS PROMISE

Grace is the power to live now as if things are going to be all right tomorrow—the third face of grace. The power, mind you, is not born from a desperate gambler's hunch, against long odds, that things are bound to get better. It is a power generated by the Spirit of Jesus, who has convincing evidence that God has a way of leading us through disaster into victory, and making promises come true. Grace is a mysterious power to live as if you *know* tomorrow will be better than today, even though common sense gives you odds that tomorrow will be the pits.

A lot of us desperately need the power to live by promise. Some of us have the feeling that we are locked in a car going full steam down a steep hill— with steering wheel locked and no brakes. Nothing can stop us. Nothing can stop us from blowing up the world in a final nuclear wipe-out. Nothing can stop inflation from choking off the livelihood of elderly people. Nothing can stop us from letting half the world starve to death in poverty and the other half suffocate in the poisoned dust of our technological affluence. We seem en route to cosmic catastrophe. But these are only the global fears, the sense that we are caught in a system that ultimately delivers disaster.

Our smaller fears hurt us even worse. They are puny by comparison, but they pin us down on all fours more quickly than the world terrors do. I make no defense for our nearsightedness. I only report that most of us feel more anxious if we suspect one of our kids is on drugs than if we hear that fifty thousand children are hungry. So we need a promise with power to give us a hope that drives out fear.

A thousand unwitting kids, as I wistfully watched, were being pushed out of high school at the point of a diploma. Some were shining salutatorians on their way to a bright future with a pleasant detour through Stanford or UCLA. But for every valedictorian who believed his or her dreams would come true, there were one hundred and fifty confused kids who had no dreams, who didn't know where they were going or how to get there if they did. Oh God, how they need a promise that tomorrow can be better than today.

Thousands of unwitting lovers, this June, while I write, will stand in front of a preacher, waiting for magic words that will lift them off into love's endless spaces where happiness is the air they breathe.

24

But for every couple ready to fly the friendly skies of love, there are a hundred couples whose flight was grounded years ago when the power of love petered out and the inertia of boredom or the energy of hate set in. How they need a promise that things will be better tomorrow even though they are rotten today.

Ten thousand unwitting new MBAs, this June, are joining the game called "getting ahead in the company," the great crusade in quest of the glittering prizes of a free economy. But for every rising young executive there are thirty thousand men and women plodding along from nine to five, bored, bruised, and boiling in jobs they never really wanted, or wanting jobs they will not get. How they need a promise that things can be different tomorrow from what they are today.

To people like these, and to every one of you who has lost touch with God's good intentions for your future, I want to repeat St. Paul's amazing word: Grace be with you—grace as a promise that, when you can barely cope with today, you can live with power to believe that things can be better tomorrow.

When common sense says that life is frozen in a black block of despair, when the pundits say there is no answer, when even theologians tell you that God has abandoned us to our fate . . . may grace be to you, as the amazing promise that your future is open to God's surprising will for your good.

Why do we call grace amazing? Grace is amazing because it works against the grain of common sense. Hard-nosed common sense will tell you that you are too wrong to meet the standards of a holy

God; pardoning grace tells you that it's all right in spite of so much in you that is wrong. Realistic common sense tells you that you are too weak, too harassed, too human to change for the better; grace gives you power to send you on the way to being a better person. Plain common sense may tell you that you are caught in a rut of fate or futility; grace promises that you can trust God to have a better tomorrow for you than the day you have made for yourself.

We would make a mistake, of course, if we expected everything to happen at once, instant, full blown. It may come in fragments, a nudge of power here and a ray of hope there. It may happen in one sector of your life at a time; do not look for the whole story to be told in one chapter. You may have it and lose it and need to get it all over again. But the Lord will open you by his grace, as you go, to new winds of pardon, power, and promise. It may be happening right now, as you read. It may come through while others are chattering around you. Maybe as you drive to work or as you stop for a light. Maybe later, in the dead of night. The fact is that the grace of God that brings salvation to all has appeared. And no matter how you got to be where you are, no matter how wretched your condition, how bad your hurt, and how drained of hope you may feel, it can be all right at the core of your life.

So come with me, then, and we will poke around in some of our sensitive spots to see how, here and there, now and then, we will understand that we are embraced by a grace that has one function in a world gone wrong, the function of making it right in spite of everything. While we look around, I think you will find yourself in places you have been before; I will only be a guide in your own home grounds. As we pass through, and look at zones of life touched by grace, I hope something inside of you nudges you to embrace the grace you feel embracing you.

who will find yourself in places you have been
before. I will only be a guide to your own inner

you discover your own resources and find joy in
engaging with.

2. You Don't Have to Live in Your Dog House!

✍ THE GIFT OF JOY ❧

This is the day which the Lord has made; let us rejoice and be glad in it.

Ps. 118:24, RSV

You and I were created for joy, and if we miss it, we miss the reason for our existence! More, the reason Jesus Christ lived and died on earth was to restore us to the joy we have lost. Jesus himself told us; all that he said to us on earth came down to one primary goal—that we should share his joy. The church officially echoed Jesus when it taught us that the chief end of men and women was to glorify God and enjoy him forever. C. S. Lewis sensed it when he remarked that joy is the chief business of heaven (and, I would add, of earth as well). So we can safely believe that when we think about joy we are at the edge of life's deepest secret. We are not talking about emotional frills and psychic indulgences; we are talking about the discovery of all-rightness in the essence of life.

If joy is our human destiny, it is also our human desire. We all want a little enjoyment. Let's not be hypocritical, as if we were too serious to want joy in our lives. Let us admit that what keeps us going is the hope that one night the bells will ring and the Hallelujah Chorus will sound for us too. I dare say that anybody who pretends to want only to serve and never to enjoy is a slovenly person, and probably a little nasty too.

An ancient verse-maker invites us to do what we were created for and what we truly want to do: "This is the day which the Lord has made; let us rejoice and be glad in it." Surely the old poet speaks the language of human longing.

So what is our problem? The problem is that we have such a ridiculously hard job doing the very thing we were created and redeemed for. Kierkegaard put it something like this: Most of us spend our lives building mansions for ourselves and when we finish we choose to live in the dog house. Or, in John Bunyan's sad figure, we lock ourselves in a cage, in the center of a dark room, and then complain that God put us there. In short, we decline the destiny of joy for which we were given this day of our lives and for which we were given the gift of life itself.

Enough reason, then, to think hard about getting out of our private doghouses, out, that is, of our guilt, our fear, our anger, our resentment, out of the doghouses of our souls, into the joy of this day that the Lord has made. Let me ask—and answer—three questions about joy, questions that stick in my own mind when I wonder where my joy has flown: *What is joy? What gives me a right to it? What prevents me from experiencing it?*

29

WHAT IS JOY?

I suspect that, to answer this question, each of us has to locate a moment in his own life, a moment of special joy, seize hold of it, examine it, and let it be a parable of joy. My own joy parable came one night after hearing a concert by Isaac Stern and the Los Angeles Philharmonic. He played one of the romantic concertos that set my heart on fire, and I was deeply moved. So were we all. We heard him. We received his gift, and when he was finished, we blessed him. We gave him the hallowed benedictions of our sweet applause. He took joy in our blessing, and he kept coming back for more. And when he came back, we took to our feet. We were swept away, beside ourselves with gratitude, and I suddenly realized that I was enjoying the applause more than I had enjoyed the concert. And I knew why.

In the receiving of Stern's gift, and in the giving of our blessing, we were enacting a parable of the meaning of life under God in this universe. We had received a truly great gift—the gift of Brahms's genius transformed by Stern's artistry. In turn, we were moved by the feelings of *gratitude* for the gift and a *desire to bless* the giver. Heaven might be fun after all—even those endless doxologies in the heavenly choir!

Joy is an intermezzo of gratitude that interrupts the routine motion of life. Our lives, for the most part, are motion and struggle. Most of us spend our time crawling, groping, climbing, sometimes running, but always moving like the works of a clock. But now and then joy comes to arrest the motion, it stops the tedious ticking of our life-clocks with the bracing discovery that we have received a gift. It works most magnificently when we feel our own life as if it were God's gift to us. Stilling, for a moment anyway, the haunting anxiety that maybe life is made only of the stuff that hurts and angers, and makes us feel small and stupid and phony, there comes a sense that life—now, here, today—is a gift worth blessing God for. When it comes, when this sense of being a gift comes, joy has come to us.

Joy is not just the experience of God, thank God, though being with him, in the sight of his beauty, will be the ultimate joy. Not the least gift of grace is our joy in creaturely things. God is so great that he does not need to be our only joy. There is an earthly joy, a joy of the outer as well as the inner self, the joy of dancing as well as kneeling, the joy of playing as well as praying. Any moment that opens us up to the reality that life *is* good is a parable of the supreme end for which we were made.

WHAT RIGHT DO WE HAVE TO JOY?

Joy is our inheritance, our birthright. It is for us only to let the Spirit open our lives to joy; we do not need to earn it. Do you doubt your right to be joyful? Then listen to the Word again. God has made your day, this day, and he has given you the right to receive it with gratitude.

This is the day! Take it, first, in its simple, literal sense. Today, that square on your calendar that marks out another block of time on earth. Today, not yesterday, not some fantasized memory of when the children were too small to make you

31

weep, when your spouse was turned on to love, and when you looked like a handsome winner. Today, not tomorrow, not some dreamed-of future when you can get out of the rat-race for good, when you are in the fifty percent tax bracket, and you finally fulfill yourself in a new career. Not a day in memory's glow, not a day in fantasy's vision, but this day, here, now, whatever its pains or problems or punishment. This is the day! God made it, set you in it, and joy in it is your inalienable right.

Take it further, to do justice to what *this* day means from God's vantage point. The Psalmist had his eye on something bigger and deeper than a Tuesday or a Friday. He was looking to Salvation Day, the Resurrection of Jesus Christ, and every new possibility for every day that flows from it. This day, then, is the life that the Lord made possible by dying and rising from death to become the Victorious Lord of every day. We are dealing here with the dawn, not of a calendar day, but of a new age, a new creation, and with it a new hope. The gift of hope is the gift of joy. It is your right because God made the day through raising his Son from a tomb and making him Lord of your day.

Now take it just one more step. When the Psalmist says that God made this day, he is talking about more than a time-frame, a square on the calendar, a hitch in life's routine. He is talking about one's very being. One's *life,* within this day, is the day God has made. Point to yourself and say: "I am the one God has made today. I am God's gift to me, and I bless him for giving my life to me." When you say it, you are letting the "day the Lord has made" have its deepest meaning. When you know in your heart that you are God's special gift to you, you know you have the trust deed to joy in your hands.

But a terrible problem about the right to joy stares us in the face. Joy may be our right. But is joy *appropriate* for the serious and sensitive Christian in our time? Is it fitting, is it *seemly* for rich Christians to seek joy while children are starving? Is it decent to want joy while we all may be drifting insanely toward nuclear disaster? Might it not be obscene to wish for joy in a world filled with so much pain? Can our joy, what little some of us have, be honest?

If our joy is honest joy, it must somehow be congruous with human tragedy. This is the test of joy's integrity: is it compatible with pain? Or is joy the cheap charade of a superficial society of lotus eaters?

Only the heart that hurts has a right to joy. Only the person who cries for the needless death of children has the right to bless God for the gift of life. You truly celebrate the gift of your existence only when you also cry out in pain for people whose existence is the constant humiliation of human injustice. You can shake your tambourine, you can speak in the ecstatic frenzy of a thousand charismatic tongues, but your noise is only self-indulgent gibberish unless your joy is tempered by the miseries of God's people around the world. I am fearful of some of our pious joy. It sounds often like *La Dolce Vita* of the saved soul, life in a sanctified pleasuredome, out of touch with the reality of other people's tragedy.

When I wonder whether joy can be a decent emotion in our world, where tragedy is endemic, I am encouraged by the impression I get from people closest to suffering. I sense a mystifying joy in Mother Teresa, whose life is married to a ministry of mercy and misery. I sense a powerful joy in Dom Helder Camara, whose life is poured out for the wretched poor in Latin America. I feel an almost tangible joy in the presence of Allan Boesak, who feels the oppression of his black brothers and sisters in South Africa.

The joy these people radiate reminds me that tragedy is not the last word. This is still my Father's world. The red sunset over the Pacific is the setting of his sun, the third movement of Mozart's *Jupiter* symphony is his music, the touch of a loving hand is his touch, and the extended hand of a crucified Savior to offer a new beginning for every failure is his hand. And so my life is still his good gift to me even amid the cries of the hungry, the yearnings of the oppressed. I have permission to rejoice even in a world of pain.

Joy also has to be compatible with the pain within me. To promise joy without pain is Pollyannaism, make-believe, deceit. Legitimate joy must be the experience of joy along with pain. And it seems to me possible. Maybe there is more joy in Watts than in Palm Springs. Maybe joy is more real lodged in the interstices of pain than as the climax of a pleasure trip. Maybe joy in this life always has to be "in spite of something." The joy of a person with an inoperable brain tumor can be infinitely deeper than the thrill of a birdie on the eighteenth hole.

The other night, trying to sleep, I amused myself by trying to recall the most happy moments of my life. I let my mind skip and dance where it was led. I thought of leaping down from a rafter in a barn, down into a deep loft of sweet, newly mown hay. That was a superbly happy moment. But somehow my mind was also seduced to a scene some years ago that, as I recall it, must have been the most painful of my life. Our first-born child was torn from our hands by what felt to me like a capricious deity I did not want to call God. I felt ripped off by a cosmic con-artist. And, for a little while, I thought I might not easily ever smile again.

But then, I do not know how, in some miraculous shift in my perspective, a strange and inexpressible sense came to me that my life, our lives, were still good, that life is good because it is *given,* and that its possibilities were still incalculable. Down into the gaps of feeling left over from the pain came a sense of *givenness* that nothing explains. It can only be *felt* as a gift of grace. An irrepressible impulse of blessing came from my heart to God for his sweet gift. And that was joy . . . in spite of pain. Looking back, it seems to me now that I have never again known so sharp, so severe, so saving a sense of gratitude and so deep a joy, or so honest.

This is why we must remember that joy is not the same as pleasure; that, while we are glad for pleasure, we live for joy; and that joy is possible even when pleasure turns to ashes. If you can have joy and pleasure, cherish them together. But joy in our world is more at home with pain. Joy, when you come down to it, is a feeling that it is all right with us even when everything seems wrong.

WHAT PREVENTS US FROM HAVING JOY?

Is joy a real possibility in our lives these grim days? Can we do something about joy? Can we prepare ourselves for it, or is it a gift that must always take us by surprise? Maybe we cannot manufacture joy. But we can decide to decline a waiting gift. We can close ourselves to joy. We can harden ourselves against it. We can be caught in the rut of life's perpetual motion. We can keep so busy that we crush joy out of our days. We can regard life as such a solemn matter that we lose even the desire for joy.

Each of us has his or her own techniques for killing joy. Let me tell you, first, how we kill other people's joy. We kill joy in others whenever we refuse to let them have joy in the giving of their gift, whatever the gift may be, or when we refuse to let someone around us enjoy being thankful for the gift. We kill other people's joy when we make them feel their gift is not quite good enough for giving.

I am going to illustrate my point with a terrible story. It is about my oldest sister and her gift to me. She is the only really talented person in my family, and her talent has been making fine clothes for people. I visited her in Michigan a while ago and noticed the handsome jacket her son was wearing. When I told him I liked the fit of it, he said: "My mother made it for me." "Splendid," I said. "Would you like me to make you one like it?" she asked me. Is it possible, I wondered. "Of course, no problem." So she took down my measurements and told me to send her so many yards of the wool of my choice. The next time I was in Michigan, the jacket would be ready. Well, with some doubt, I did it; but could it possibly fit?

A few months later, some duty brought me to Michigan—I hardly noticed what it was, my mind was on the jacket, and the fear of her disappointment if it did not work out well. I was in the living room of my mother's home and could see my sister drive up, get out of her car, walk up the front steps with the gold jacket over her arm. She came in; we exchanged pleasantries, but not for long, for the suspense was killing me.

I put the jacket on. I turned around, front, sideways, back. I looked in the mirror. And I saw that it fit; wonder of wonders, it fit; *gloria in excelsis Deo,* it fit. I could see the light of joy in my sister's eyes. She had created her gift and given it to me. I wanted to take her hands and dance a jig of gratitude around the room. But then—and this is the terrible part— my mother's voice fluttered from a stuffed chair in the corner: "I don't like the color."

Something inside my mother needed to kill the joy. Now, I dare mention my saintly mother in this connection only because I know that if she could kill the joy of someone dear to her, so can I. Just find one plausible reason why someone around you should not simply be glad to give and glad to receive—whatever it is he has to give or whatever it is she opens her eager heart to receive. Let that single reason, justifiable as it is, smother the marvelous moment of giving and blessing, and you will kill the joy. And when you kill joy, you snuff out life's most lustrous gift.

Now let us talk of killing joy in ourselves. I think we all have our own joy-killing demons. Let me—at the risk of indiscretion—tell you the names of my three worst joy-killers.

The Lust for Virtue.

This is the demon that whips people with a suspicion that they may not be virtuous enough to deserve joy. It drives them to an insanely futile quest for the virtue that will entitle them to believe that it truly is all right with them. But virtue is not the route to joy. The dumbest heresy ever circulated among the elect is that virtue is its own reward. I can confide to you that I have personally survived several severe attacks of virtue—and it was never a reward. Virtue enough to deserve joy is only a mirage. It is always beyond reach. And your search for it only drives you into the desert of despair.

Virtue demands too much of us. Trying to be virtuous enough to merit joy is like trying to hold up the world when you have no place to put your feet. The effort drains you of the very joy you want to earn.

For that matter, what most of us lusters after virtue want is not to be virtuous, but to have reputations thereof. And since we can never be sure of our reputations, we are deadly afraid that someone might see our flaws and discover we are frauds. Lust for virtue is always the seedbed of deceit and anxiety. What is even worse, we may actually be stupid enough to believe in our own virtue and, in the delusion, make asses of ourselves and bore our friends to death.

Lust for virtue is the denial of grace in our lives. And the denial of grace is the most fatal of all joy killers.

Total Accountability.

Some of us nurture an illusion that we are accountable for all the ills of the world. In our silly pride, we are stupid enough to suppose that God expects us to carry on our little backs a load that only Jesus can bear. But total accountability is the special demon that besets sensitive and moral people. It seduces them to feel full responsibility for every oppressed person, every hungry child, and every victim of racism. If they are parents, they insist on feeling accountable for everything their grown children do, accepting guilt for their failures and taking credit for their successes. The more sensitive you are to other people's troubles and your own responsibility, the more vulnerable you are to the demon of total accountability and the more likely you are to forget that only God is infinite, and that we are only finite.

There is a wonderful story about Pope John XXIII. He was being hounded by a serious cardinal to do something decisive to resolve the unsolved tragedies of the modern world. The pope put his arm around his curial nag and said that he too knew the temptation to accept total accountability for the whole world. He was personally helped, the pope said, by an angel who came to him at night in the papal bedroom and said: "Hey there, Johnny boy, don't take yourself so seriously." Frankly, I often need a genial angel like Pope John's.

Problem Catastrophizing.

My third demon is in charge of making me inflate problems to the size of catastrophes. It makes me feel that every time I have a nasty problem, calamity has befallen. God turns catastrophes into problems; my demon tempts me to see mere problems as gigantic catastrophes. If you share my demon, we have a common kill-joy. You overdraw your checking account, and you face financial disaster; you learn that your daughter smoked pot, and your children are ruined; you have one rousing fight with your spouse, and you are ready for a divorce. When our demon prevails, we lose our balance; the demon unhinges us.

Some of us are catastrophic hypochondriacs. Every pain in the chest is the coronary you were worrying about, every case of the flu is probably deadly pneumonia. The demon called hypochondria steals joy and sets panic in its place.

My oldest son, when he was very young, tended to be a histrionic hypochondriacal problem-catastrophizer. He cut his cheek one day and saw the blood drip to the floor and he panicked: "I'm dying, I'm dying." Then, with a sense of timing that would have done Bob Hope justice, he paused and cried, "I am already dead!" Well, an interjection of rationality into the situation persuaded him that anyone with such a superb sense of the dramatic was probably in the land of the living. But the hypochondriacal demon gets into many of us; and when it does, it kills our joy.

Some of us are spiritual catastrophizers. We do not just make mistakes, we are not satisfied to admit that we blow it once in a while; when we fall into a sin, we are spiritual wastelands. One failure and it is better that a millstone be hung around our necks. When I get into this joyless abyss, my demon speaks to me in the language of King James: "Oh thou feckless fop of a man, surely there is no spark of spiritual strength in thee; fie on thee, fatuous wretch, for such a worm as thou there is no hope." Then God comes and puts it in perspective: "Watch it, friend, you have a bit of a problem with that temper, haven't you? Let's work on it together." The joy-killing demon will paint every spiritual fault as final reprobation, every problem as hopeless catastrophe. The Lord turns the catastrophe back into problems we can cope with.

So out with this demon! To catastrophize our problems is to capitulate to chaos and to deny that God is at work in our lives. The Spirit calls us to believe that real catastrophes can be turned into problems with the help of God. So how stupid it is to feel like ultimate wrecks when we have only tested and seen that life can be a bit tough.

I do not think we can earn the right to joy. Joy is always a gift; it comes from the Spirit of Joy. But we can recognize some of our joy-killers and we can let God exorcise them.

Maybe the worst mistake we can make is talk about joy instead of letting it happen. Dostoevski makes this point in his story about "the dream of a ridiculous man." This is my version of the tale. Once there was a wretch of a man who decided to punish everyone around him by committing suicide, the final way to get even. He set aside a night for making his quietus. The night having come, he loaded his handgun, sat at his miserable table, made his mental preparations—and fell asleep, pistol at his elbow. Soundly sleeping, he dreamed a marvelous dream.

He was swept off to another world, one much like ours, except that people there were different from us in one important way: they were joyful, always, all of them. The dreamer watched them and wondered. How could they have such joy? He went to the men and asked for the secret of their joy. And each man answered, "Joy? We do not know what that word means." He went to the women: "Please tell me the secret of your joy." "How can we tell you when we do not know what you are talking about?" He went to the children: "Why are you joyful?" And they smiled at him and told him they could not understand his strange words.

So he learned that people who have joy do not need to understand it. They just *are* joyful. But then the dreadful thing happened. He stirred them up so much with his questions that they began thinking about joy. They began talking about joy. They began discussing it together till late into the night. They paid scholars to take sabbaticals to write theories about joy. They blabbed about it incessantly and began to write songs about it. The dreamer noticed, to his horror, that while they talked, they lost their joy. He had caused their fall!

So the dreamer, seeing the monstrous thing he had done, began to preach to the people that they had made a great mistake, they had fallen into despair. "Do not talk about joy—you can *be* joyful. Do not write about joy—*be* joyful. The important thing is not what you *think* about joy. The gift of joy is at your door. Take it!"

And the people, who had, in their innocence, been possessed by joy, said to him: "You are a ridiculous man and your talk is the dream of a ridiculous man." They went back to their harangues. Some despaired of life and fell into death. They had traded the reality of joy for words about joy.

At another time and another place, another man, Jesus, came and spoke to us of many things. When he was about to leave, he said: "These things I have spoken to you, that my joy may be in you and that your own joy may be abundant" (John 15:11). And now his Spirit comes to us with the power to believe that joy is our birthright because the Lord has made this day for us. When we have power to *accept* our day as his gift, we have entered our mansion of joy and discovered one more way that it can be all right even when everything is sadly wrong.

3. You Can Gamble on a New Beginning and Win

❦ THE GIFT OF FORGIVENESS ❧

If we confess our sins, he is faithful and just, and will forgive our sins . . .

1 John 1:9, RSV

Michael Christopher's powerful play *The Black Angel* haunts everyone who sees it with the most painful question short of our own death—the question of forgiveness. What do we do when we forgive someone? What do we receive when we are forgiven by someone? What happens between two people when one forgives and the other is forgiven? And why does it take a miracle to pull it off?

Christopher's play is about a former German army general named Engel who tried to make a new beginning for himself and his wife outside a little French village. He had been in prison for thirty years, sentenced there by the Nuremberg war crimes court. Now (incognito, he hoped, and forgotten) he was building a cabin in the mountains. His own past, with its horrendous guilt, was forever behind him, paid for by three lost decades in prison. He would try to forget it all. He had earned the right to a new beginning.

But a certain French journalist named Morrieu could not forget. His family had been massacred in a village that Engel's army had overrun during the early days of the war. Every last person in the village had been shot to death by Engel's soldiers. No, Morrieu could not forget.

For thirty years he had planned revenge. If the Nuremberg court could not sentence Engel to die, Morrieu would pronounce his own death sentence. Now, after thirty years, the time had come. He went into the village to stoke up the embers of hatred and fear in the minds of the village radicals and crazies. He did it well, for they made plans to go up the mountain, burn the cabin down, and assassinate the former general.

But Morrieu had some lingering questions, and he wanted answers from Engel. So he went to the cabin the afternoon before the night of vengeance, introduced himself to a shaken Engel, and spent the whole afternoon in a terrible inquisition of the old man. He had to get the whole wretched story straight, in all its details, before Engel died with his secrets. But as the afternoon's probing dialogue wore on, Morrieu's taste for revenge began tasting sour. After thirty years, for the first time, Morrieu had doubts; he plunged himself into Engel's soul and tore his own soul in pieces. Morrieu changed his mind. He warned Engel of the villagers' intention to attack that night and offered to take him to safety.

The general waited a long minute before responding. He would go, he said, on one condition: that Morrieu forgive him. Morrieu found himself unable to do that. He could save him, but never would he forgive him.

That night the villagers came as a mob. They walked in the cowardly courage of the faceless mob, courage given by hoods that covered their miserable faces. They burned the cabin to the ground and shot Engel and his wife dead.

The play left us gasping for an answer to the question of forgiveness. What was it that Engel wanted more than life itself? What was it that he needed so badly that he would rather die than live without it? What was the one thing beyond vengeance that Morrieu did not have the power to give? What is this miracle we call forgiveness?

Listen again to the promise of the word of God: "If we *confess* our sins, he is faithful and just, and will forgive our sins . . ." The word tells us that God can be counted on to forgive; it is about God's unfailing freedom to do what Morrieu could not. But God's forgiving is a model of what can happen between two alienated human beings. The dynamics are the same. God shows the way.

Notice the close connection between confessing and forgiving. "If we confess, he forgives." You will make your life miserable if you force these words to say more than they do. The Bible does not, it simply does *not* say that if we do not confess we will not be forgiven. It only says that if we do confess we most surely shall be forgiven. What God does with unconfessed sin is the private affair of his infinite mercy. We deal here only with the assured, the guaranteed, the no-risk promise. "If *we* confess, *he* forgives."

Since confession is the first word in the dialogue of forgiveness, we must ask two questions instead of one. What is a confession? And, only then, what is forgiveness?

WHAT IS A CONFESSION?

Confessing sin is not the same as talking about sin. If talking about sin were the same as confession, our society would be on a confessional binge. No people on earth has ever let it all hang out the way we do. Celebrities race each other to the publisher with their secret sins, steaming manuscripts under their arms, rushing to tell their own private gossip to a nosey public. Fortunes are made on the conviction that we have become a nation of peeping toms. I have listened to a talk-show psychologist on my car radio and marveled at the willingness of people to divulge their private peccadillos to their show-biz therapist and to the few million people who happen to be eavesdropping. But blabbing our secrets is not the same as confessing our sins. Spilled beans do not a confession make.

Second, confessing sin is not the same as explaining our sins. I am usually more than willing to explain my faults. I want everyone to understand me, and to appreciate the extenuating circumstances that led to my most understandable mistakes. I want you to know that I am not a terrible fellow; I am really only a victim of some unfortunate neuroses. If you only knew the disadvantages

47

of my childhood, if you only knew how uncontrollable my passions are, you would understand the crazy things I do. I can explain everything. That afternoon on the mountain, General Engel did some profound explaining; Morrieu should know what it was like to have been a general under that idiot Adolf Hitler. Explanations, yes, but no confession.

Third, confessing sins is not the same as being realistic about sin. If realism were the same as confession, we would be the champion confessors of all time. No people has ever been so willing to pay good money to see the seedy side of human nature, eyeball to eyeball, without blinking, as we are. Dr. Karl Menninger wrote a book a few years ago called *Whatever Became of Sin?* In it, the well-known psychologist called us back to honest realism about sin. But as I paged through the book, I noticed two missing words: confession and forgiveness. Realism makes us honest, it makes us tough, it makes us real. But realism about human sin is only a prelude to confession, and it does not open the door to the miracle of forgiveness.

Well, if confession is not the same as blabbing, not the same as explaining, and not the same as being realistic, what is a confession of sin? I believe that confession includes three ingredients, and if we miss any of them, we have short-circuited our confession.

First, confession is an acknowledgment of our responsibility. Let me concede to you that, as I get older and see more tragedy, I grow more convinced that people are often more sinned against than sinning, more often victims than culprits. We are victims of many forces, and no one can tell us just how much our own wills are responsible for what we decide to do. I do not know how much you can blame on the anemic genes and chromosomes you inherited, or on the fouled-up psychic training they foisted on you in your childhood. But I am sure of this. Somewhere within the personal dynamics of the wrong you do, somewhere inside the working of your mind and will, you make a choice for which only you can give an answer. You chose, you acted, and you are accountable. It's not my father, not my mother, and not my early toilet training, it's me, O Lord, standing in the need of prayer. And I have not confessed unless I accept responsibility for the wrong I do to my neighbor or to my God.

Second, confession is a shared pain. When I truly confess to you that I have hurt you, I am saying to you: "The hurt I caused you now hurts me too. I feel the pain I inflicted on you. I wounded you, and now I am wounded by the cuts that I sliced into your life. I share your pain." Only when pain is shared can confession begin; a painless confession is a sham and a contradiction.

Sharing the pain we have made other people feel does not come easy. This pain is, in fact, the one we defend ourselves against with the fury of a hornet in front of its hive. And our defense is almost sure. The hurt I caused her, after all, was sweet justice, nothing less. Well, vengeance maybe. But she had it coming in any case. Why should she not feel it all? Once I had screwed up my courage to tell her the truth, I knew I was pure in my fury. She's done more than her share, after all, to make me miserable. So when I finally let her have it, I went for the jugular, I only balanced the pain scales. Oh, yes, what I did was get even. Nothing more. So I feel no need to feel her pain. Why should I?

So it is that we build barricades against our own guilt, and it takes time, and amazing grace, to crawl through our defenses far enough to get a fix on reality. I have injured a soul, child of God, fragile human, and left her bleeding in my wake. Maybe someone will help me see at least the fringes of what I did, see how savage my lust for the pleasure of her pain, how mean my vengeance. If I get this far I may allow myself a dull disgust for my wretched assault against her.

But I must go further if I want to confess to her. I must imagine what it was like for her to be bludgeoned by my unshackled fury; I need to feel what it was like for her to feel my vicious words shoving her into a horrible cellar of unlovedness—yes, for the moment even, of hate. When I begin to smell, then to taste, the venom of my own vengeance, I am nearly competent to confess. Take your time, let the pain another felt at your hands, your voice, your meanness, gradually seep into your soul. When it gets there, you will—with the honesty of shared pain—be able to speak those miraculous words of healing, "I'm sorry."

Third, confession is a gamble on grace. What a risk we take when we confess! And how high the stakes can be! How can you be sure that the person you hurt has enough of grace's power to forgive you? How do you know, after you have held out your sorry soul in your hands for him to see, that the other person will not look at its unmasked ugliness, and slam the door on your face? When you confess, you admit that another person has reason for turning against you; only the power of grace can prevent it. What a risk!

In Thomas Hardy's classic *Tess of the D'Urber-villes,* Tess is a young bride who gambles her happiness, her very future, on her new husband's power to be gracious. She risks everything by telling him, on her wedding night, about a tragic mistake in her past relationship with another man. As she confesses, his body stiffens, his lips become tight, his dry eyes freeze in a blank stare. He has no grace powerful enough to forgive. She gambled on his love, and lost, and her life was over. Confession is a gamble on grace.

A confession, then, includes acknowledgment of your own responsibility, the experience of shared pain, and a readiness to gamble on grace. With these, any confession can be the beginning of a miracle that tears down a wall that alienates you, and can build a bridge you can walk across to each other's forgiveness.

What, then, is the miracle that happens between two people after one confesses and the other forgives?

WHAT IS FORGIVENESS?

There are at least two things that forgiveness is not.

First, forgiveness is not forgetting. Forgetting is not hard, and it is not painful. We forget what does not matter much for us anyway. You need no miracle of grace to get you to forget. All you need is a bad memory, or *maybe,* a fear of reality so intense that you stuff the ugly pain of the past into the dark pit of your unconscious. God does not forget; if he could have forgotten, he would never have taken on the cross of Calvary. Forgiving is not forgetting; forgiving is remembering and still forgiving.

Second, forgiveness is not excusing. We all deserve a lot of excusing for the crazy things we do. Extenuating circumstances! If you understand all, you excuse all! Anyone with an ounce of empathy is willing to suspend judgment on me once he understands my condition. Goodness knows, my wife simply has to excuse me because she understands me so well. She knows I forgot to keep my promise because I was working too hard. (We workaholics always have an edge; we deserve to be excused because we are so virtuous.) She understands that I was a pain in the neck last night because I had to finish an essay on forgiveness; so she will let me off the hook. Excusing is not really terribly hard. It makes for tolerance. "You are a flake, but you're my kind of flake." "My husband is a clod, but with the mother he had to grow up with, what could you expect?" Excusing is an end run around the crisis of forgiving. It is a way of telling a person he does not need to be forgiven after all.

What, then, for God's sake, is forgiveness? If it is not forgetting or excusing, what is it? What happens when God forgives a sinner? What happens when a hurting person forgives the person who caused the hurt?

Forgiveness, at bottom, is a very simple sort of miracle. Forgiveness is a new beginning. Forgiveness is starting over and trying it again with the person who caused you pain. Take God, for instance. When God forgives, he offers us a new start with him. He holds out his hand and says, come on, take it, I want to be your friend again. In spite of everything, I want to be with you, and I want to be under you and over you and in you, as the loving power of your existence. I am not going to let anything you do get in my way. So let's begin again. This is what God does when he forgives—he breaks down the walls we build and gets into the backyard of our souls to make a new relationship.

We do it too, with each other. You start where you are, not where you wish you were, not where you would be if you could rearrange life, but wherever you are, now, with any person who has hurt you, and you make a new beginning. You hold out your hand and say, I want to be your friend again. I want to be your father again, your daughter again, your lover again. Let's start over. This is forgiving.

The miracle of forgiving is the creation of a new beginning. It does not always take away the hurt. It does not deny the past injury. It merely refuses to let them stand in the way of a new start. You do not have to understand why he did it. You do not have to get the whole story straight, to sew all the loose ends together so you can be sure there are no secrets left. You certainly do not have to squeeze every ounce of guilt from the soul of the person who did you wrong. You just begin where you are in your shared pain. You both hurt, and so you make your shared pain the starting line of a new relationship.

And you walk together into the future. What future? Who knows? All you have is a new beginning; no guarantee of where it will end. The future is going to bring more pain, you can be sure of that much. More confession, more shared pain with people who hurt you. More new beginnings. We never stand still.

Again, you start where you are. Some of us have to forgive people who are beyond our reach, and we have to begin with them on a totally different basis. You may have to forgive a former husband who still hates you so much he would stuff your forgiving spirit down your throat. You may have to forgive a neurotic mother long dead, and begin again with only a memory of her. Forgiveness does not deny the past; it can only create a new future. Sometimes we can only forgive in absentia, letting go of our resentment and spite, and starting over with the free spirit inside of us, leaving the other person to God.

This miracle of forgiveness is so hard to perform that you may wonder why you should even try. Once you have been stung by somebody's brutal unfairness, you have gale force motivation for never forgiving, never, never, never. The logic of sheer justice is stacked strong on your side. It is not fair to forgive. He did the dirt. He made you feel so foully unlovable that you felt less than human. All you owe him is your contempt. So let him feel the frigid blast of your scorn. Why should he get anything from your hurting heart but a lash of hate? Let him sleep in his own dung! Use your holy right to the one kind of clout you still have with him—the clout of your contempt.

Why should you forgive him?

There are only two good reasons, I suppose. They may not add up to a fair deal on your calculator, but they do add up to freedom and power in your life. So check them out.

The first reason is that the biggest loser in the getting even game is the person who cannot manage the power to forgive. You never know for sure how much you hurt people by not forgiving them. But it can hardly be as much as you hurt yourself. When you make a hard decision against forgiving, you lock yourself in a straitjacket of your own resentment. You get boxed into a house haunted only with horrid memories. Unrelieved resentment is like a videotape inside your soul, playing its tormenting reruns of the rotten things somebody did to you, playing it over and over, wrenching your soul tighter every time it plays. You get hooked into it; you become a hard-core addict and you cannot leave it alone. Your resentment has you shackled to the everlasting pain of a raging memory. Your only hope is to find the freedom of forgiveness.

The second reason for forgiving is that, when you forgive someone who hurt you, you are dancing to the rhythm of the divine heartbeat. When you forgive you are in tune with the music of the universe. You are riding the crest of love, the energy of the cosmos. God invented forgiveness as the only way to keep his romance with the fallen human family alive. If God had not found inside himself the power of love to forgive, there would be no future for the likes of us. But he found it—and the hope of the whole world is vested in his readiness to make a new beginning with us, a million new beginnings if they are needed. So every time an ordinary person discovers the power to begin again in a relationship with someone who caused him needless pain, he walks in stride with the living God.

As a matter of fact, freedom to forgive flows out

to us precisely when we feel him forgiving us. So get in touch with the source. You can depend on it. God has taken the risk out of confession as far as he is concerned. With anyone else, forgiveness is still a gamble. But he is faithful and fair, always, to forgive, to make a new beginning with us at a moment's notice.

What makes the difference? The difference is a wooden cross dug into a hill where a man once died in shared pain for the sins of the world. On the cross, Jesus gathered all the pain we made God feel, and he felt it there with God. He felt the same pain God feels when we turn our backs on him and chase after the silly tin gods of our own making. Shared pain, between Jesus and God; this was his way of confessing our sins for us. Speaking for the human family, Jesus, in his pain, was saying: "We're sorry, God." Shared pain, it happened there, and now God is totally faithful and fair to make new beginnings with any of us who care to have him on our side.

There is a cross of shared pain in the life of God. This is why he never shuts the door to us. You can bet on it; he will always forgive. He does not merely forget, he does not merely understand; he puts himself at our side and says, "Let's start over. I will be your father. I will be your friend. I will be your savior. So let's get going."

"If we confess, he is faithful." Never mind that your confession is not perfect; it never will be. All our confessions are faked a little, half-baked, half-intelligent, and half-sincere. There is a fleck of the phony that sticks to all of us, even when we try to come to terms with God. No matter. God's forgiveness comes through anyway because the pain we caused him was perfectly shared by our brother Jesus. So we must never let the tarnish on our own confessions keep us from enjoying God's forgiveness.

GOD'S FORGIVENESS AND THE FREEDOM TO FORGIVE

I think there is a connection between feeling the force of God's forgiving us and finding freedom to forgive others. Two dialogues come to mind that illustrate the connection between God's forgiveness of us and our freedom to forgive people who hurt us. The first one is about God's forgiveness as the only answer to ultimate despair. The second one is about our freedom to forgive once we feel forgiven by God.

Dialogue One.

One of the most moving conversations in human literature can be found in Dostoevski's *The Brothers Karamazov*. Two brothers, Ivan and Alyosha Karamazov, are talking in a tavern about the insufferable evils that people commit against each other, especially against children, in our broken world. Ivan, the atheist, argues with white hot passion that there is no way in heaven or earth to have harmony between God and this rotten world. Alyosha, the simple believer, cannot fashion an argument to counter Ivan's ferocious indictment against a God who tolerates man's inhumanity to children. Silent,

with his face in his hands for many minutes, Alyosha finally stutters the only answer available to
anyone. "There is one," he said, "who can forgive
everyone everything, because he shed his innocent
blood for everyone and everything."

Dialogue Two.

After the Second World War, with the scars of Nazi
brutality still crusty on her soul, Corrie Ten Boom
felt called to preach forgiveness to all Europeans as
they dug out of the war's emotional rubble. She was
sure that she had overcome her own desire for
vengeance against the S.S. troops who had dehu-
manized her and her loved ones in the concentra-
tion camps. Her ministry once took her to Munich.
On a Sunday, outside the church, she found herself
looking hard in the face of an old S.S. guard who
had watched and sneered at the frightened women
prisoners while they were forced to take delousing
showers in front of him at the camp. Suddenly, it
was all there again, the roomful of mocking men,
the pain and the shame of it. Now, the war over, the
man came up to Corrie, beaming and bowing.
"How grateful I am for your message, Fräulein. . . .
To think that, as you say, he has washed my sins
away."* He put out his hand to her. It was too much
for her; she kept her hand frozen at her side.
Forgiveness comes hard for anyone; it seemed outrageous to expect it of her. She tells us how, at that
moment, the angry, vengeful thoughts boiled
through her system. She struggled to raise her hand.
She could not. She felt nothing, not the slightest
spark of forgiveness. So she breathed a silent

prayer. "Jesus, I cannot forgive him. Give me your forgiveness."*

Corrie was touched then and there by the One who can forgive everyone everything. She somehow felt forgiven, and in the freedom of being forgiven she raised her arm and took the hand of the man who had done unforgivable things to her.

And there, I believe, is the heart of the matter. When we are freed by forgiveness we learn to freely forgive. And when we forgive, we are free. We are free to make a new beginning and thus know, in our hearts, that it may be all right again even when someone has made everything unspeakably wrong for us.

---

*Corrie Ten Boom, *The Hiding Place* (Washington Depot: Chosen Books, 1971), p. 215.

4. All the World's a Critic, and You're Tired of Reading the Reviews

❦ THE GIFT OF FREEDOM ❧

With me it is a very small thing that I should be judged by you or by any human court. I do not even judge myself. . . . It is the Lord who judges me.
1 Cor. 4:3, 4, RSV

One of the fine arts of gracious living is the art of living freely with our critics. When we have the grace to be free in the presence of those who judge our lives and evaluate our actions, we have Christian freedom. And, feeling free, we feel as if things cannot be all wrong.

We will always have critics, of course. There is no escaping criticism. Critics are all around us, some welcomed, some self-appointed nuisances. They size us up, take our measure, weigh us in their scales, and form their own opinions of our lives. They may approve of us. They may think we are walking disasters. They may think we are too conservative, too liberal, too easy-going, too serious, too wicked, too saintly. They may be right or, on the other hand, they may be wrong. But they will criticize; they will call us to account before the bar of *their* judgment.

Each of us has at least three critics. There are three judges who stand at the front door of our lives; each of them is adding up our assets and subtracting our deficits in the computer of his mind. We cannot live without them. The question is, can we live with them?

Your first critic is your neighbor—anyone who is important in your life. Your mother, perhaps, or your father? Your friends? A pastor or a teacher? They judge you because they care about you; they may love you or despise you, but they care. If they did not care they would not bother to criticize. And you care, too; if you did not care about them, you would not care about their judgment of you. This makes living with critics hard; we care too much. If your critics are getting too hard for you to please, or if you sometimes feel that there are too many critics in your life, too many people to please, know this: grace can set you free from your critics.

Your second critic is your own self. We are gifted with the unique power to get outside of ourselves and be our own judge and jury; this is the blessing and burden of being just a little lower than the angels. We may be our best critics. We may be our worst critics. But we cannot stop criticizing ourselves as long as we are genuinely human. When you take your seat in the critic's corner, you take on a job that definitively separates you from all lower species. But being our own critic has certain job-related risks. We can become nags instead of critics, and nags are a pain in the neck—even if they are the nags in our own heads. If you feel weary of dragging along a nagging suspicion that you haven't measured up to your own impossible standards, know this: grace can set you free from your own self-judgment.

Your third critic is someone you cannot see, but who sees you only too well. His name is God, and he is your toughest critic. It is not popular to talk about God as judge these days; the fashionable God is all grace and no judgment. Judgment is old-fashioned, nasty, vicious; people today want a God who not only loves unconditionally, but approves of us unconditionally. But being graceful does not make God less critical; grace does not blind God to what is going on, nor does grace make him less honest in calling things as he sees them. Someone asked a modern theologian if he still believed in divine judgment. The answer came: "With things the way they are, I don't believe in anything but judgment." A little one-sided, maybe, but enough to make it sound reasonable to say that God is still our critic. This means he has expectations of us by which he measures our performance.

What God expects of us, says St. Paul, is that we be faithful. He puts us on earth as caretakers (or stewards, in older English). He put each of us here to take care of something. And what he asks of us is that we be faithful in taking care of it. Something there is in life for each of us to care for. He does not ask that we be flawless, only faithful; not fantastic, not fabulous, only faithful. Being faithful means to find out what you are here to take care of and then give it your best shot. And God is your critic. If you have trouble living with this critic, know this: grace can set you free in the presence even of your divine critic.

Let's begin with the critic out there—your neighbor. St. Paul, almost off-handedly, declared his own freedom from human judgment this way: "With me it is a small thing that I should be judged by you or by any human court." He was telling some meddlesome Corinthian Christians to get off his case, but we can adopt his stance as our own.

Freely translated, it comes to this: You will evaluate my conduct and you will make an assessment of me, I know, and when you do I will listen to you. I know that you will size up my work; when you do, I will consider what you say. I know that you judge me because you care about me; so I will care about what you say. What you say and what you think about me matters to me. But I want you to know that after I have wrestled with my own conscience, after I have consulted my own convictions, and after I have made my decisions, your judgment will not matter much. It matters some, but not much. I will not let your appraisal tell me how to feel about what I am and what I do. I will not rest my case with you.

Is this really St. Paul talking? Is this the St. Paul who told members of the church to be willing to give themselves as servants to fellow Christians? Is this the St. Paul who reminded us that God gives us pastors, counselors, and parents to help us know who we are and what God expects us to do? Is this the St. Paul who urged us to subject ourselves to each other in loving care? Yes, the same apostle.

He is not a fool, you know. He does not say that he cares nothing for the feelings of other people. He

63

himself was ready to become all things to all men. But not to *please* them, only to win them. He says, When it comes to my deepest self, my own way of life, I have got to put your criticism on the back burner and live my own life before the Lord. I will not be intimidated. I will not be condemned. I will not be damned by other people's judgments. I will be free.

What freedom there is here! What power! What joy! When you do your task in life as best you can, when you know you are in touch with your own conscience, when you have prayed about, thought about a tough decision, and you have finally made up your mind, and you go ahead with a free spirit no matter what anyone else says or thinks, then you finally have found a precious freedom.

Your critics may be right, of course; they may be smarter than you are, and know something you don't know. So if you are wise you will listen to them. But when you *believe* you are right, and your critics think you are wrong, you can set their criticism somewhere in a far corner of your mind, and be free from it.

It is self-inflicted brutality to live under the tyranny of other people's judgments. It makes you very sad to live your life only to please other people. Not long ago, I met a beautiful woman of about fifty who looked as if she had just stepped off the pages of *Vogue* magazine—bright, talented, and educated. She had tried to commit suicide. She came to her fiftieth birthday and realized she had lived her entire life only to please other people, terror-stricken that she might let them down, be criticized by them, and lose their love. At fifty, she discovered she had lived a half-century in the prison of other people's opinions. A wise counselor led her out of prison into freedom. Some people remain children and prisoners all their lives, trying to please their mothers, or other little gods, for fear that if they do not please their critics they will be lost.

Many of us have very special people in our lives whose judgment of us is very important. I lived for years under the shadow of a beloved professor whom I revered as a student; I think I would have voted for him if he had been a candidate for the job of God. I wanted him to be proud of his student. It took a minor miracle for me to spring free enough from his judgment to be able to say in my heart, "It is a small thing to me what you think of this book I'm writing."

Whom do you live to please? Whose criticisms get you down and make you feel guilty? Who unsettles you and leaves you shaken when they judge you? Whoever it is, you are invited to shake yourself free and say: "What you or any court of human opinion thinks of me matters some to me, but, in the crunch, it doesn't matter much."

So that takes care of the critic out there—other people. It leaves us with our cruelest critic, the one inside, our own selves.

St. Paul took the measure of his own self as critic and, with a heroic nonchalance, said: "I do not even judge myself."

Come now, old man, surely you jest. We heard you say once that you were the *chief* of sinners. If that is not judgment, I have never heard it. And you have given some of us fits of self-doubt with your

65

own words telling us to examine ourselves. "Take time with yourself," you told us, "see what is happening to your life, ask where you are going, be sure of what you really believe, know what your dreams are for your life." You are not a fool, surely not a smug, complacent, self-righteous conceited fool. Don't claim too much, apostle.

I can hear St. Paul rescue himself from my cavil, "Yes, of course I examine myself. But I know how wrong I can be. I know that if I decide I am innocent, I may be wrong. And if I decide I am guilty, I may be wrong. So I cannot take my judgment too seriously. If a man who pleads his own case has a fool for a lawyer, the person who accepts his own sentence has a fool for a judge."

St. Paul knew that we are our own worst critics, not because we are very tough, but because we are very tricky. We are subject to too many moods. Some of us have lucky rose-colored glands that make us look beautiful in our own eyes. Others seem to have a foul chemistry inside their blood that makes everything bright in their lives look grey to them, and everything grey look black. We cannot trust our judgments. We either excuse ourselves too easily or we accuse ourselves too harshly.

Some of us even con our own consciences; we excuse ourselves for anything. I once found a student cheating. According to him, he had such a horrendous headache, the professor was such a bore, the test was so unfair, and his parents were nagging him so relentlessly to get good grades that he not only had a right to cheat, he had a solemn obligation. Vice presidents of large companies are sure that they owe it to America to bribe foreign customers in order to get contracts. I have spoken to prostitutes who feel they should be thought of as social workers engaged in a street ministry for alienated males, on the night shift. There is no limit to our ability to con ourselves into easy excuses for our lives.

But we are just as likely to scourge ourselves three times a day with a moral whip. We feel guilty as charged even before the trial begins. The guilt often has nothing at all to do with the real quality of our lives. One of the West's great jurists, Hugo Grotius, father of modern international law, summed up his self-evaluation as his last words on his deathbed: "I have done nothing worthwhile with my life." This judgment had no resemblance to the monumental fruitfulness of his life. I know people who are too busy doing good during the day and too tired at night to do any fancy sinning; and yet, if you went by their feelings about themselves, you would think they were a combination of Jezebel and Rasputin. We can wallop ourselves, never know a day free from our own judgment, and be completely off target in our judgment.

People as guilty as Beelzebub can come off feeling like happy saints. And saints who spend their lives helping other people can come off feeling like the befouled fallen of the earth. So only boneheads will trust the judgments they make about themselves. We need grace to put our own self-criticism on the comic pages of our lives. We need to say with Paul, "I do not even allow myself to judge me."

One more judge is waiting in the wings. But look

who's here! Have we leaped out of human frying pans into the flames of God? It's the critic up there—the Lord God himself.

St. Paul rests his case here. He stops short before the one judge he cannot put on the back shelf. "My judge is the Lord." Is this good news or bad news?

Before it can be good news, it has to sound like very bad news. To run smack against a judge who never compromises and never makes a mistake could be terrifying. Consider a picture of our affair with God as we get it from Psalm 139. Is this the sort of God into whose judgment you want to fall?

He is everywhere. "Where shall I escape from your spirit?" the Psalmist asks. The answer? Nowhere. Not at the edge of the earth, not in the outer darkness, not in the suburbs of hell. If I run away from him, he is ahead of me. If I pull down the blinds, he sees through them. If I try to escape while he sleeps, I discover that Jehovah neither slumbers nor sleeps. If I sneak away in darkness, he is light itself. There is no hiding place; wherever I am, he is there too.

He knows everything. The Psalmist says: "You have searched me and known me. . . . You know my thoughts. . . . You know my words before I get them on my lips." He has us wire-tapped. He knows our motives, our plans, our excuses. Whatever it is, he knows. Nietzsche wrote a story about a man who in desperation killed God. They asked him, "Why in the world did you kill God?" The answer: "He knew too much." This is bad news, to know that *he* is your judge!

To make matters worse, he gives us all the

chances in the world to make mistakes. He pushes us into a world that has potholes in every road, pitfalls at every corner. And he gives us so much freedom. Decisions! Decisions! Decisions! And always, this all-knowing God stands in the critic's corner.

It could be too much. With a critic like this, we need to come to terms. We certainly cannot stand up under his judgment; it will condemn us. We have two choices.

First, we can make believe he is not there. Lots of people do this. They simply live as if he did not exist, or as though he died a while back, maybe when the scientific age was born. They are the fools who say in their hearts that there is no God. This is one option; live out the fantasy, act out our lives in the illusion that he is not really here. This may actually work for a while, but not forever, because sooner or later the illusion will be shattered and the reality will be known, that God is alive.

There is only one other way we can live freely in the presence of our infallible critic. We can get to know him for what he is really like. This was Paul's secret; he knew his divine judge in a way that made him free. For he met him at the cross. The secret of what happened there was that our divine judge judged his own Son in our place. There, his accusing finger, once pointed at us, was changed to an open hand outstretched to us. His terrible swift sword was exchanged for his supporting arm. Our judge became our divine savior. Our critic became our best friend. Now the last word is grace—the pardon, the power, and the promise of grace. God is on *our* side.

And this is why I can, with all due respect, tell my human critics to mind their own business. I can learn from other people, but I do not need to spend my life trying to please them. I can learn from myself, but whenever I feel the incriminating judgment of my perfectionist conscience, I can laugh at the judge inside myself. For I have a divine judge who has the final word and he has become my friend. When he criticizes, I know he will say: "But it's all right." I know that there is "now no condemnation," no condemnation at all. I am free.

To be free in front of our critics is only one way to know that it is all right when everything is all wrong. Some of the worst seizures of all-wrongness come on us in the shape of guilt. We can feel all wrong when important people condemn us, or when we are afraid they may. We feel all wrong when our own conscience slaps us with a guilty verdict. But when we feel God's "It's all right," we can at least begin to feel that it's all right with us where it really matters.

5. You Can Still Be Wonder-Full in a Wonder-Killing World

✍§ THE GIFT OF WONDER ৯৯

> . . . Each one heard them speaking in his own
> language. And they were amazed and wondered. . . .
> But others mocking said, "They are filled with new
> wine."
>
> Acts 2:6-7, 13 RSV

One thing about my father-in-law, he knew how to
buy the right kind of Christmas presents for his
wife. Year after year, he gave her exactly what she
wanted. He never missed; his batting average at
buying the right gift was one thousand percent. He
always knew ahead of time that when his wife
opened a package from him she would find in it
precisely what she knew she wanted. His method?
Simple. She went downtown to the department
store and picked out whatever it was she wanted for
Christmas that year. Then she told her husband
what it was, down to the model number and the
store salesperson to get it from. Then he would go
to the store and do his Christmas shopping, have
the thing wrapped in bright holiday paper, and his
job was done. No risk. No anxiety. And no surprises. He used the flatiron approach to Christmas

shopping: you iron out all the wrinkles of uncertainty, but you also flatten the peaks of wonder and surprise.

My daughter, when she was small, had a very different approach. I used to watch her tantalize herself with tickles of curiosity about the packages under the Christmas tree by the stairs in our living room. She would poke around until she found the packages marked for her. She would pick one up in her hands and squeeze it gently like a careful shopper feeling for ripe tomatoes. She would shake it softly, with deliberate care, then hold it in both hands to feel how heavy it was. When she finished this solemn ritual, she would slowly put it down again. She would have given heaven and earth to know what was in the package. Yet she wanted above all not to know what was in it, because she wanted a surprise later on. She wanted to know; but she was willing to stay in the dark for the sake of surprise. She wanted to wonder, to respect the mystery, until the marvelous moment of revelation.

Inside of me the spirit of my father-in-law and the spirit of my daughter are wrestling for control. They contend for control of my attitude towards life in general. On one side, there is the flatiron attitude. I hate to take risks; I hate to admit that I don't know what is going on. I want to keep things under control around me; I want an explanation, no surprises please. There is inside of me a wonder-killer. But I also like surprises, I want to keep wonder alive, I love it when my jaw drops, my eyes pop, my knees shake, and I am reduced to amazement. I want my life to be wonder-full. I think that Jesus Christ invites us to transcend our lust to have everything under control and be lifted to the mind-boggling experience of wonder.

Pentecost was just the sort of thing to awaken both the wonderers and the wonder-killers. Some wonderful things happened at the birth of the New Testament church when the Holy Spirit came. Crowds had come from many foreign places to celebrate the Jewish holiday in Jerusalem, and a lot of people were milling around the temple on the very day of Pentecost. Suddenly, an eerie howl came up like a fierce gale whistling through the mast of a sailing vessel; but the air was becalmed. Torrents of little flames fell down from somewhere above onto the shoulders of Jesus' followers; yet there was no fire. Some of the disciples began to speak out, and the people—who understood only their own native languages—held on to every word that was said. These were the signs of the coming of the Spirit, "great things and full of wonder in our ears," as Milton called them.

These strange and exotic happenings excited two responses. In one group, people were awe-struck. We read that "they were amazed and wondered" that simple Galileans, speaking their own native dialect, could be understood by people who had never heard it before. These were the wonderers. Another group was more realistic; they figured there had to be an explanation and they would know what it was. These were the flatiron folk. They had a compulsion to iron out the peaks of wonder because they could not stand the thought that something was happening that they could not control. So they hit on the explanation: "These men are drunk, loaded, bombed out of their minds. This explains everything." Never mind now that their logic was crazy, as if drunken speakers explained the power of listeners to understand them. Just notice the flatiron attitude. Flatten the peaks of wonder so that you can keep everything in order.

Jesus always creates a crisis of wonder when he comes. Wherever he appears, he confronts us with the deep question of whether we want to approach life the way my father-in-law approached Christmas, with no risks and no surprises, or whether we are willing to keep wonder alive, as my daughter was able to live with Christmas packages before Christmas came. Will we sometimes join the people at Pentecost who saw a miracle and gasped in wonder? Or will we always be among those who must have an explanation for everything? Is there any wonder in our lives? Or are we compulsive flatironers? Jesus challenges us to leave some room for wonder.

It happened when he first came on the scene in a manger of Bethlehem. The shepherds were struck with terror at the blazing angels sashaying around the Judean hills. In their wonder, they rushed to the mangerside to see the child. Again in wonder, they ran out to tell their friends. And we are told that "all who heard it wondered at what the shepherds told them." The flatiron mentality had not gotten to them yet.

So it was his whole life through. As a boy, he engaged in dialogue with learned men, all ripe with scholarly "ifs" and "buts"; but, we are told, they wondered at him. He boggled people's minds all his life. Common people saw him, and sensed that there was more to him than met the eye. Common sense said, "We see only a carpenter's son." But he said: "If you see me, the carpenter's son, you are looking at God." And when he said it, people wondered.

The apostles who wrote about his life were impressed with the people's amazement. Listen to their recital of the wonder he awakened: "And when Jesus finished these sayings, the crowds were astonished at his teaching" (Matt. 7:28, RSV). "And they were astonished at his teaching" (Mark 1:22, RSV). "The multitude was astonished at his teaching" (Mark 11:18, RSV). "And all who heard him were amazed" (Luke 2:47, RSV). "And they were astonished at his teaching" (Luke 4:32, RSV). "And they were immediately overcome with amazement" (Mark 5:42, RSV).

But just as he inspired awe and wonder in some, he also brought the flatiron thinkers out of the woodwork. The Pharisees wanted to live in a world neatly under the control of a God who did everything their way. We can explain everything, they said smugly. There is really no mystery here. He has a devil inside of him; he does miracles by the power of Beelzebub. This does not help modern flatiron minds, of course, since they believe that the devil expired when God died. But it seemed to explain things for the ancient flatiron mind.

The woods are full of wonder-killers today. Sometimes I suspect there is an international conspiracy against wonder organized by the flatiron thinkers of the world. They pop up everywhere. Let me tell you three of their primary haunts, the places where they hang around to wring the neck of wonder and wipe out amazement from our world. Their favorite haunts are television, technology, and theology.

Today's television specializes in wonder-killing. If tv is bad because of its sex and violence, it is a far more serious menace for its killing of wonder. It uses creative genius to flatten out all the peaks of life; it is a billion dollar industry created on the premise that there is nothing more to life than what meets the eye. A few utterly predictable laughs from sit-coms. A little standardized violence, plus a smidgen of banal sex, and that is all you get. No real surprises; Shirley and LaVerne are going to be as dumb next week as they were last week—you can depend on it. The first rule of tv is: strip life of its deep mystery, let the flatiron mind that worships Nielsen ratings take away the peaks of wonder.

Technology also creates open season for wonder-killing. Ironically, technology kills wonder by means of its own wonderful achievements. At first, technology boggled our minds. Then we began to believe that technology can control everything and explain everything. Thus the very wonder of technology destroys the wonder of life. A mechanical device sails around the planet Venus, sends pictures back to our tv screens, and the average American says, "What else is new? Turn M*A*S*H back on." A baby can be conceived immaculately, not in the virgin's womb, but in a test tube; not by the Spirit, but by a pair of gynecologists. The wonder of human conception is covered over with technology. Masters and Johnson put sex into a laboratory under scientific control and take the mystery out of it, making sex less naughty but more routine. An awesomely horrible thing happens in Jonestown, and soon after, reporters are trying to wring an explanation of the massive horror out of experts on human behavior. I want to scream, "Don't take the mystery, don't take the wonder out of this hellish evil; I demand to let this awesome horror be a mystery that no one can ever comprehend. I want some wonder left in my world."

Then there is theology, my home field. Once the job of theologians was to protect the mystery of the Christ from heretics who wanted to explain it all away. The heretics were the flatiron folk who had to have an explanation for how God and humanity could be joined in the man Jesus. Theology said: Don't try to explain it; believe it and wonder at it.

Later, theology turned against the wonder it was hired to protect. Flatiron theologians do not like strings left untied, knots left stuck, questions left dangling. So they batten the hatches of our minds and tighten the mainsails of our beliefs. I recall how some of us first responded to the charismatic movement. Some people leaped for joy and said: "I was healed; it is a miracle." Flatiron theologians said: "You *cannot* have been healed; according to our theology, healing miracles had to stop when the apostles died." Do you sense the wonder-killing syndrome? We have our system; and by heaven, our earthly systems will not allow any surprises to upset them. Wonder is killed by flatiron systems.

Jesus Christ is a declared enemy of the flatiron mentality of our time, or any other time. Where Christ comes in, the doors of life are open to wonder. When you meet him, you know that great chunks of life exist that cannot be wrapped snugly inside a blanket of rational explanation. When he meets you, he opens you again to wonder.

What the Gospel offers to our *faith* is mind-boggling mystery. We cannot respond to the incarnation of Jesus Christ merely with rational theories of time and eternity. "Fall on your knees, O hear the angel voices"—this is the way of wonder.

Behold the Great Creator makes himself a house of
   clay,
A robe of virgin flesh he takes, which he will wear
   for aye.
Hark, Hark, the wise eternal Word like a weak
   infant cries!
In form of servant is the Lord, and God in cradle
   lies.

This is the poetry of a faith unafraid of wonder. How can we suppose, once we encounter Jesus Christ, that we live in a world where wonder has been sewn up tight in a rational sack and buried under a heap of technology?

The grace that came to the world with Jesus offers to our *experience* a life of mind-boggling wonder. Grace comes as a marvel of pardon when I think I have fouled out of God's game forever. Grace comes as a surprising power when my common sense tells me I cannot cope with my life. Grace comes as a miracle of promise when everything in my world says that life is hopeless. "Amazing grace, how sweet the sound that saved a wretch like me"; let that old song settle in your heart and you can never close your heart's door to wonder again.

Keep a door open to wonder and even the ordinary people around you will take on an odd dimension of mystery. Every person you know will be a potential eye-opener. You may meet people you do not like, but you will never again meet a person you can take for granted. Wonder kills stereotypes. All the people clustered around you—people bound to you by routine loyalty, others floating at the fringes of your inner circle—they are all awesome folk, each one hiding a mystery far too deep for the likes of you to have all figured out.

Beware the flatiron minds of the world who piteously pretend to unravel the riddle of the free human spirit. Those behaviorists, for instance, who seductively convince the scholarly gullible to give up on personal freedom and dignity, to trade in the family of free persons for a population of manipulated bundles of conditioned reflexes—what are they afraid of, these wonder-killers of the human psyche? Are they not afraid that there really is a mystery in each of us, a mystery that may pop up and thumb its nose at a know-it-all psychologism just when it seemed to have killed our wonderous humanity? But I do not want to take on the wonder-killers of psychological theory; I am willing to leave them to play with their pigeons in the labs of universities. I want to talk instead about the wonder-killers inside our own minds.

You have to admit, don't you, that you don't really expect anything new and exciting from old George. Have you not gotten your husband, after all these years, almost stuffed into a mold of minimal expectations? But, then again, maybe you have been blinded to the potential for mystery in the person you've lived with for twenty years. It is there, even if you are mystery-blind. Take your children, too. After reading the manuals on effective child-rearing and all those sure-fire magazine pieces on child psychology, have you not settled in on a pretty confident sense that you have scoured the inside of your own children? Or, if you have not gotten them fixed in your head, you expect that some expert should be able to do it for you? But the fact is that even your children are profound mysteries, not because they are slightly crazy, but because they are thoroughly human.

We tend to treat our parents, especially if they are getting on, in the same way—as if they are empty of surprises, as if there is no more mystery within them. Be careful, they probably are hiding secret selves inside who strain at the leash to get outside and stick their tongues out at people who took them too quickly for granted. One of the dumbest ways to relate to elderly parents is to let them know that you understand everything. They may be laughing at you on the inside, and wondering if you could cope with some of their secrets.

If we could get tuned to wonder in other people, we may also be ready for the mystery of our own selves. There is more to me than meets my eye, and more to you than meets yours. You have not even begun to unravel the mystery of your self and your mind; you are deep, unfathomably deep. You cannot be a shallow person; God does not make shallow people. You can, if you choose, close your own mind to the depths within you. But you cannot be shallow.

This is ten thousand times clearer if you are a

Christian. Consider this wondrous self-discovery. Can you see yourself this way and still suppose that you could be a shallow, predictable person: "I live, yet not I, but Christ lives in me" (Gal. 2:20)? There is the mind-boggling truth about you; Jesus Christ, in his Spirit, present in you, without shoving the real you aside, at the depths of your existence. When you look in the mirror, you should get your eyes off your midriff and look into your own soul and see yourself as a deep, wonderful mystery of God-likeness. Do not let the flatiron wonder-killers of the world destroy your sense of wonder at the mystery and marvel of your very soul.

It takes grace in our time to keep our minds open to wonder, to be ready for the tug from God, the push from the Spirit, and the revelation of deep things from the hearts of ordinary people. It takes grace, but it is a great gift. If you have a place in your life where your eyes can still gape, your knees quiver, and your mind boggle, you are open for wonder. And, open to wonder, you are ready for God's surprises, even the greatest of all; that it can be all right when everything is wrong.

You may be able, when the dark sky falls upon you, when life is skewed, your situation off center, you may just be able to see what others cannot see, at a level below any they guess existed. In spite of everything, you may be able to know that you are all right inside the hands of an invisible but wonderful God. You will miss this saving sense if your heart is closed to wonder. So let there be wonder in your life! Blessed are the wonderful, for they shall see God, and they alone shall know themselves.

6. When You Hurt with Hurting People, You Are Dancing to the Rhythm of God

◆§ THE GIFT OF SUFFERING §◆

. . . If children, then heirs, heirs of God and fellow heirs with Christ, provided we suffer with him.
                                    Rom. 8:17, RSV

A friend talked to me not long ago about an unusual worry simmering on the back burners of his conscience. Life was treating him well. He had a lovely wife and a pretty good marriage. He was in good shape, strong as a healthy ox. All his children were beautiful, talented, and doing well. He had won star status in his field of work. So what was he worried about? He was worried that something might be wrong if everything was this good.

I should tell you that he was a Christian, too, and knew that Jesus led his followers to expect things to go wrong sometimes as a consequence of their commitment. But he had not suffered, not much anyway. Where did that leave him? Was there a soft spot in the underbelly of his Christian commitment? How could it be all right with him when everything was going so well?

About the same time, I was jolted by what must

be the Bible's toughest word on suffering. It goes like this: we are children of God—along with Jesus—*provided* that we suffer with him. It is the small print in a footnote of the Gospel—only sufferers need apply. There is no heaven for us unless we suffer with him on earth. Maybe my friend does well to worry.

If we have to suffer to qualify as children of God, some of us will need to revise our vision of the good life. Most of us look at suffering and wonder, *why?* Jesus tells us to look at suffering and wonder, *why not?* Most of us think of suffering as something we should avoid at all costs. Jesus expects us to choose to suffer with him as the smallest price to pay. If we refuse, we are not his friends and we are not the children of God.

Put it as plainly as it can be put: we need to suffer some of the cussed wrongness of life in order to find its deep rightness. We have to feel pain we do not want to feel, carry burdens we do not want to carry, put up with misery we do not want to put up with, cry tears we do not want to shed. If we feel no hurt now, we will, when all is done, be the most miserable of all people. Ultimately, at the end of the game, when we cash in our chips, it will be all right with us only if we have been hurt with life's wrongness.

There is a catch 22, however, a most crucial catch, and we had better know it. It is not as if any old suffering qualifies us as the children of God. It is not as if it will be all right merely because we have been walloped with the bare fist of fate. The catch is that we have to suffer *with* someone else who suffers. Why not put it concretely and Christianly? We need to suffer *with Jesus*. We are "fellow heirs [of God] with Christ, provided we suffer with him." This is the catch. Some catch!

So before we talk about differences in suffering styles, let's agree on what suffering is. Try my simple definition. To suffer is to put up with things you very much want not to put up with. If you badly want to be rid of something and it will not go away, you are suffering. It may be only a nuisance—a fly buzzing madly in circles, never landing anywhere in your bedroom, when you are wild for want of sleep. It may be a guilt whose sting you feel until you die— the memory of having betrayed a spouse. Suffering can be a physical pain, like a headache or bone cancer. It can be mental anguish, like the desperate loneliness that sets in when a loved one dies or the ache we feel when our child goes off the deep end alone. What marks any human experience as suffering, and what binds us together in a fraternity of sufferers, is a powerful desire that our pain, our grief, our hurt go away, and we have no power to make it go. Suffering, just any kind of suffering, then, is a feeling that things are wrong with us and we cannot make them right.

But there are two ways to suffer. Two ways, like alternating currents, negative and positive, intertwined, meshed, inseparable, but different. There is the way of suffering *from something*. There is the way of suffering *with someone*. Suffering *from* and suffering *with!* A heaven and earth lies between them, when it comes to quality. Let me show you the difference.

We suffer *from* something when pain comes to us, grabs us in its claws, crushes us, unwilling, captive. It can come from nature or it can come from people, it doesn't matter which. Wherever it comes from, suffering attacks us. It is a tricky enemy, it sneaks up on us, we are never really prepared for it, it whams us when we think everything is fine. It worms its way into our lives, unnoticed at first, like a lump in the chest the size of a pinhead. Sometimes it wallops you head-on, as word that your husband was just hit by a truck. Sometimes it just keeps annoying you, in short seizures, like an unsupported hunch that your wife is having an affair. We suffer from nature when we get a pinched nerve at the bottom of the spine or a metastasis in our guts. We suffer from people when we are cheated by a crook, betrayed by a friend, neglected by a lover. No matter what hits us, when we suffer *from* it we are being victimized. It is unwanted, uninvited, loathed; we never choose it. We bear it only because we have to, stuck with it like a damned spot that just won't come out.

Nobody, I suppose, gets through life without suffering from something or other, or somebody or other. But suffering from something does not land you in the kingdom. You are not a naturalized citizen of the kingdom of God just because you have been cuffed by cruel nature or crummy neighbors. But then neither are you locked out just because you were lucky enough to have escaped.

We could go crazy if we really believed we had to suffer from things as a qualifier for heaven. I could imagine an epidemic of pious masochism. Healthy people, lucky in love and all good fortune, might feel secretly gypped if they were denied the advantage of suffering. Morbidity? Consider the other side of the coin. People who have been clubbed down and dragged along by ills that would make anybody shudder may congratulate themselves for having bought a first-class reservation in heaven with the price of their awful pain. False hope? I could only want them to be right; some people suffer enough here to make it seem obscene for them not to get happiness afterward.

There is no guarantee, though; hurting does not make us sure winners. I'm sorry about that.

But so much for suffering from things; we need to get on with the heart of the matter. Suffering *with* people! We suffer with people when we choose, freely, to let their hurts hurt us. Forget about being a victim; here you decide for yourself whether you want to be hurt or not. We are free in this suffering, free to suffer or to run, free to take on pain, and free to say NO to it. We do not hurt now because nature whops us; we hurt only because we choose to share the hurt nature lays on other people. We bring it on ourselves, it is our doing. We make our move, get close to sufferers to let their pain seep through their skins into our hearts until their pain becomes our pain. Here, in the irony of chosen pain, we decide to accept a pain we want to do without, we will to be hurt with a hurt we would rather not feel, we choose to bear a burden we want very badly not to bear. This is suffering *with;* it is the last word in love's power to move toward our neighbors, not to get pleasure from them, but to get hurt with them.

Suffering *with* someone does not hurt any less than suffering *from* something. The difference is not in the amount. The difference lies only in the will. In suffering *from* something, we simply receive it, nobly or meanly, with heroic courage or ordinary cowardice, but we do not choose it. In suffering *with* somebody, we take it into our own hands to suffer. We choose to do what we do not have to do, or even want to do; we walk, eyes open, into the pain of another human being and claim it as our own.

It must be transparent to anyone who knows the life of Jesus that he was a genius at suffering with people. Suffering *with* is what was wholly unique about how Jesus suffered on earth. He certainly suffered a lot, and he certainly suffered *from* the hands of other people. He suffered from the rage of frightened bigots. He suffered from the cool cruelty of imperious Rome. He suffered from the facile fade-outs of his friends. He suffered from hard nails in his soft skin. And yet, he did not suffer uniquely as the Savior of the world because he suffered a lot. There have been other great sufferers besides Jesus, and we do not need to prove that his pain was much worse than the pain of people who were burned at the stake after they had their fingernails slowly pulled from their fingers. What was special about Jesus' suffering was not the quantity, but the quality, not how much he suffered from others, but how he suffered with others. It was suffering *with* sufferers that made him a Savior.

Jesus still puts himself into the shoes of anyone who suffers. If you want to know who the vicar of Christ is, find yourself a hurting human being in your neighborhood. Jesus is found where people are putting up with things they want to go away, trying to cope when everything is all wrong. He is represented on earth by the wounded. He is not among them as a visitor, not even as a comforting friend.

He *is* one of them; he is any or all of them. Talk about transference of one's identity; in his mind, Jesus becomes the human sufferer.

Jesus points to suffering people and says, "There I am." He says it because he feels it. He feels their hurt and, in the sharing of pain, equates the sufferer with himself. Jesus *is* your hurting neighbor. He *is* your hurting child. He *is* your hurting enemy. He is anyone who is suffering *from* anything not of his or her own choosing. If you feel the hurts of any person who hurts, you are suffering with Jesus. Listen to him if you doubt it:

> If you visit a man in jail, you visit me. If you put clothes on a naked person, you clothe me. If you give a hungry person something to eat, you feed me. If you linger at the bed of a sick person, you linger with me. If you open your door and invite a stranger in, you invite me. (Matt. 24:31–46)

This is Jesus talking.

But I never saw Jesus. Did you? No matter. Jesus says: "I tell you this: anything you did for one of my brothers here, however humble, you did for me" (Matt. 25:40, NEB).

The cat is out of the bag now, for sure. St. Paul says we must hurt with the hurts of Jesus if we expect it to be all right with us in the end. And Jesus tells us how: we hurt with him when we hurt with any neighbor, near us or far away. We hurt with Jesus if we hurt with our husbands, our children, our neighbors, or the stranger in another land.

So the secret of personal all-rightness comes to this: love's power, this time love's power to suffer with other people. No nonsense now about liking it; we want no holy masochism masquerading as love. You have to hate the hurt, want it to get the hell out of your life, for it to count as suffering.

Let's have no foolishness about suffering being nice after all because it makes us saints. We are talking about real suffering, and suffering is not liking what you've got. But the power of love gives a person energy to choose it anyway, simply to share it with the person who is stuck with it. You choose it and you stick with it, you twist and turn, you hang by your fingernails, you wish to God it would go away, but you choose to feel it as long as the other person feels it. That is what love does to you.

Where do we locate someone to hurt with? Shall we poke around a bit, in old familiar places? See what we find?

Let's try marriage. Anybody's marriage is a harvest of suffering. Romantic lotus-eaters may tell you marriage was designed to be a pleasure-dome for erotic spirits to frolic in self-fulfilling relations. But they play you false. Your marriage vow was a promise to suffer. Yes, to suffer; I will not take it back. You promised to suffer, only to suffer *with*, however. You get your share of suffering *from*, willy-nilly, thrown at you. You *promised* to suffer *with*. It made sense, because the person you married was likely to get hurt along the route, sooner or later, more or less, but hurt he or she was bound to get. And you promised to hurt *with* your spouse. A marriage is a life of shared pain.

(Mind you, now, you did not vow to suffer *from* your spouse. If some clod of a husband hurts you by bashing you about, bodily or spiritually, put a stop to it, now. Jesus does not want you to be a conjugal door-mat.)

But a woman who is living inside a husband's pain while he is slowly, surely, devoured by cancer knows what suffering *with* can be like. Maybe it hurts her worse than it hurts him. Maybe she wants it to go away more than he does. Sometimes, as the months hang long, she may wish he would hurry up and die, get it over with, and leave her to grieve and be done with it. Maybe she resents his staying so long, lingering half-dead, while she dies a little every living day.

It is hard, this suffering with, when it lasts too long. No sweet hypocrisy please, no hankering after single-minded positive thinking. Let there be ambiguity! The point is that, in spite of the negative feelings that creep inside her heart, she chooses to feel his hurt with him. She does not shut her feelings off, she does not deny the pain. She feels the worst of it, and still sticks with it in love, real love, the love that suffers long. How long? As long as the other person suffers.

The chance to suffer with a spouse is not always handed to us from someone clearly credentialed "Sufferer." A husband does not always broadcast his pain. Maybe he expects his wife to be an extra-sensory pain-reader, to sense his hurt without his having to admit it. Maybe he disguises his suffering. The cry of pain muted inside a wordy anger, the hurting heart beneath a laughing face, the trembling fear beneath a fuming bravado, the quaking underneath a calm—a person has to have a sensitive

90

seismograph to feel some of these subterranean tremors in a pain-prone spouse.

If you suffer with somebody who fakes his hurts, you have to suffer with him as he is—a dedicated hurt-hider. You can't wait until he "gets in touch with his feelings," as we therapy-wise folk say. You can't wait until he feels strong enough to trust you with his pain. You may have to suffer doubly—with the pain he hides and with the pain that comes from hiding it. What makes it tougher, you may have to suffer with him without ever getting any credit for it; hurt-hiders do not let you know that they know you are feeling their pain. And, worst of all, it can last the life of your marriage. For goodness sake, come to terms with your role as unsung sufferer; don't make him blab about it before you are willing to feel it with him. You may have to share a pain you only guess is there. And you may have to share it a long time.

Suffering with a pain-hiding spouse is a fine art. None of us has it down pat. But even a fumbling amateur qualifies as a sufferer with Jesus.

Then there are our dear children, our most likely opportunities for suffering with Jesus. Blessings from the Lord, of course: happy is the person who has a quiver full of them. The Psalmist said that, and I will not test his sincerity, except to say that I think he said it before his own kids had reached the age of discretion. A couple of months ago, my nephew and niece let us sit through a videotaped performance of their baby's very first diaper change, filmed in the hospital, the best show in town, starring a gorgeous baby's dirty bottom. If a diaper change is a media event, the first word to come from the baby's mouth will rate prime time. But when my delirious young kin brought forth that firstborn, they unsuspectingly enrolled in the college of parental sufferers. The loveliest baby on earth is a summons to suffering by the fifteenth year, often long before. When you conceive a child, you covenant to suffer.

(Mind you, again, suffering *with* is not the same as suffering *from* our kids. Children can drive us out of our minds with pain. They do not let our dreams for them come true. They can act like subhuman savages, crush our insecure parental egos, break a hopeful heart. One slightly nutty teenager can hang the greatest soul out to dry. This is not suffering with—though it could be the occasion. One simple test for telling the difference: whenever you feel that your son or daughter is a pain in the neck, you are probably suffering *from,* not *with* him or her.)

Let me give you a modest example of suffering *with*. About a year ago, my son Charley decided to transform the motor of his ancient VW into a customized super-engine. He had only a novice's notion of the laborious adventure ahead of him, but he began buying the parts of a new engine one by one—a new carburetor, then a distributor, next a condenser. Finally, many months later, all the parts were assembled, and his completed engine stood shimmering in his bedroom like a fantastic piece of contemporary sculpture. Next came fitting it into the car itself; at two o'clock one great morning, the new engine was gingerly maneuvered into place. Once in place, the engine developed an inevitable series of minor problems—an oil leak here, some short circuits there—postponing endlessly, it seemed, the marvelous moment. Finally, the day loomed. One last fine tuning of the carburetors was needed before he started the most coddled VW engine in California; so he towed the car on a Monday to a specialist's garage, rested it in the garage parking lot overnight, and waited for Tuesday afternoon, when he would finally turn it over and move it out. A year's scrimping, a little swearing, and a lot of sweating would come to a glorious climax with a twist of a key and the heavenly roar of the magnificent machine.

It was not to be, not yet. During that last night, the most miserable wretch in the human race broke into the car, ripped off every bolted- or screwed-on piece of that splendid engine, and left a bare hunk of metal block. You do not have to be assaulted by cancer or a heart attack to suffer. Charley suffered that day, and you had better believe that his mother and I suffered with him. We shared his fury, his rage at being ripped off, not just robbed, but assaulted, shorn of something close to himself. We entered into his heart and felt his deep desire to wring somebody's neck. And when we suffered with him, in a very simple way, we suffered with the Lord Jesus.

But it is easy to suffer with a son or daughter in crisis. The crisis is caused by someone else; you and your child can take a bead on the culprit and mow him down together. You feel no threat to yourself; your own noble parenting is not in the scales. Your empathy just flows with the adrenalin.

In fact, a crisis of suffering is a neat chance to demonstrate the tender love you really have hiding inside.

Suffering with gets harder as the pain gets older and digs a trench for itself inside your child. Pain sometimes stews like an inactive volcano, hot, down deep, and always a threat to erupt, but out of sight unless you are looking down over the rim. It is tough to suffer *with* your child while he suffers in secret, hides his hurt, shows only the fury and the rage, tough to suffer with him when he rips your heart with the buckteeth of his spite. He makes you his victim, and you long for someone to come and suffer with *you*. How can you suffer *with* him when you suffer *from* him?

Maybe he gradually sinks into the black hole of his despair, ashamed of himself for being a loser, without hope, without joy, without power to climb out. You have sense enough to suspect that he is stricken, hurting, caught in some kind of adolescent hell, but all he lets you see is the foam atop his agitated resentment. You know he loves you, but all you get from him is hate. You try to get close, but all he wants is for you to stay outside. You pray in the night, and you get only silence from on high. You do not even begin to understand. Gradually you find yourself defending yourself to yourself; you have not been a bad parent, you will not take the blame. As you grind your teeth in self-defense, you begin to lose the edge of empathy for your son, you turn your pity on yourself. Suffering *with* is hard.

Oh God, you know how hard it gets sometimes, especially when some dumb-headed parent sticks her son, the winner, in front of your nose. Why can't you make it easier for people who are trying to suffer with people they love?

Then there is the neighborhood. When I think of suffering with the sufferers of the world, my mind does an educated leap to those skinny little girls we see in the ads for World Relief, children of a world far away. And I am sure there are no sufferers anywhere that compel us to suffer with them as irresistibly as hungry children do. But something happened to my own neighborhood lately that brought suffering with Jesus just a little closer to my home. Let me tell you what happened.

Our neighborhood is a quiet, decent place, lined with middle-class ranch-style stuccoed houses whose prices have shot up so high that none of the people who live in them could afford to buy them now. But there is an older house in the next block to ours, with a ramshackle look about it. It is big, ten bedrooms. It had been empty for a little while after a large and bustling family moved out, but it was rented now to some Christian people to use as a rehabilitation home for troubled young men.

The idea was to house ten or twelve men, ages ranging from eighteen to twenty-four, on their way to what they hoped would be a new life. They had one thing in common—trouble living with their own families in their own homes. Some had gotten into drugs, a few had been in trouble with the law, none of them had life put together. But all of them wanted a new beginning, and hoped to find it here at the home, where they would live under discipline, and where they would all pay their way and pull their weight to keep the house looking good.

Their presence in our neighborhood violated the zoning laws. And there was, of course, a question of property values. Would our houses lose their value if one of them was a center for healing the bent minds of a dozen troubled men? Will our girls be safe around here anymore? A fair question. Many neighbors were scared, some hysterical. Petitions went the rounds: "Get the group out of our neighborhood; save our property. Save our daughters." Most neighbors signed.

A few neighbors felt a delayed impulse. They began to think of the parents who had gone through hell with their sons, and now began to feel a nudge of hope that their prodigal had found a place where he could get his life together with God. They began to feel into the old hurts and new hopes of these parents, and began to suffer with them, with the young men, too, in their painful struggle. Their fingers could not grab a pen to have them evicted from the neighborhood. Maybe this, too, was just a smidgen of suffering with Jesus.

My wife, my kids, my neighbors down the block? What happened to global vision? There must be more important ways to do our suffering *with* people. Let's talk about the beggars along the urine-streamed curbs of Calcutta. Or maybe the oppressed victims of institutional violence in Guatemala. What about the starving children of Uganda? Sure, why not, of course; we need to get beyond bourgeois limits. Suffering *with?* That's what revolutionary priests like Dom Helder Camara and compassionate nuns like Mother Teresa do—identify with the poor by joining them. Next step, maybe, moving out of that stucco-crested block and into the stinking guttered ghetto where people *really* hurt. Why not? But for now, stuck in suburbia, Jesus' brothers and sisters are the ones joined with us by that wonderful bond of loyalty and love called a family. And if we begin there, we are at least getting practice for the big game. Crawl, then walk; that's what I mean.

Play the melody one more time. We can count on being children of God only if we choose to suffer with his hurting children. Translate: it can be all right with us, at the bottom, only if we experience the all-wrongness other people have to feel.

Easy to say. I am too tired, sometimes, to carry somebody else's load. How do you expect me to feel the world's pain after I've tried all week to sell a few Buicks to a public that wants the lousy little imports? How can I feel with my wife's anxiety when I have this rotten cold? Besides, sometimes I just don't know how. How do I suffer with my daughter's depression when she yells at me to get lost and leave her alone? I'm too tired, Jesus. And I'm no sixty-dollars-an-hour psychologist.

Where do we get the power to feel another person's hurt, keep feeling it for a long time, no relief in sight, when we have enough pains of our own? We need more love than we have. But God is love. So we need God. Why deny it? We need God if we want to move beyond our own tiredness and clumsiness, move into the life of another, not to get pleasure from her, but to take her pain into us. And there, I've said it all. If we cannot do it without God, it means we do it with God if we do it at all. So when we do suffer with someone else, even a little, we may be sure we are moving on the wave of God. We are doing what God does.

God's own answer to suffering is to join it, feel it, hurt with it. A sufferer screams to God in the all-wrongness of his life, "Why have you abandoned me?" God answers by joining him in life's most horrible wrongness. Jesus hangs on a cross and, somehow, God hangs with him. God joins us and gets himself hung for his trouble.

So when I want to share someone's suffering, I can know it is all right with me in the middle of his all-wrongness. This is why: when I get inside the life of another person, and feel her pain with her, I am on track with the ultimate meaning and power of the universe. Never mind that I do it poorly. Never mind that I don't like doing it at all. When I stick with the outrage of another's pain, I have joined Jesus. And that makes it all right with me. I have begun to be saved. I am an heir of God. It is all right with me, even though everything may be all wrong.

One day, we hope, God's way of suffering with us will end. "He will wipe away every tear from their eyes" (Rev. 21:4, RSV). Everything will be right. OK, that's hope. For now, we discover our all-rightness only if we wet our cheeks with the tears of people who are still crying.

7. You Are Only an Earthen Vessel, but God Has a Market for Cracked Pots

☙ THE GIFT OF BEING ORDINARY ❧

We have this treasure in earthen vessels to show that the transcendent power belongs to God and not to us.

2 Cor. 4:7, RSV

You are qualified to be the bearer of God's greatest gift to the human race. This may not be the greatest compliment I can give you, for he sends his greatest gifts in plain brown wrappers. His greatest treasure comes in vessels of common clay. He shows his grace through very ordinary faces. Still, it is mind-boggling to know that the face of God may be the face you show to your neighbor.

We have this treasure in earthen vessels. We are the vessels, of course, each of us individually and together—common lumps of clay carrying the greatest gift ever given to the human family. God packages and distributes his divine gift in ordinary, very undivine humanity, so that we will not admire the wrapping so much that we discount the gift.

We are the vessels; what is the treasure?

St. Paul tells us that the treasure is "the knowledge of the glory of God in the face of Jesus

Christ." The knowledge is always a knowledge of experience; it is not a head-trip, though it certainly includes the mind. But to know God is to experience him, to live with him, to be loved by him and to love him. To experience the *glory* of God is to experience God's excellence, his splendid essence; it is to know the secret of what God is really like.

Where do we experience the glory of God? We see hints of his glory in the trembling hosts of heaven, no doubt. We hear rumors of his glory in a thousand symphonies. But if you want to experience what God is really like, if you want to know his glory, you see it in the face of a man—his name is Jesus.

The face of Jesus? We must think of more than the image he could see in a pool of water, more than the cheeks down which a tear could run, more than clear Jewish eyes that never flinched in fear or shame. The face of Jesus is the living profile of a human being at work among the people who needed and cared for him. The face of Jesus means all that he was to people, all that he said, all that he did. The life of Jesus, in totality, or in detail, the tears of sadness, the sighs of weakness, the miracles of power, the words of truth—this is the face of Jesus. All this is what he meant once when he said: "Anyone who has seen me has seen God the Father" (John 14:9, NEB).

But we see the features of God most sharply if we focus our lenses on three pivotal points in his human presence. The first is his birth. The second is his death. The third is his resurrection and ascension. These three moments give us the sharpest definition of the glory of God.

In the birth of Jesus, we see God coming in weak and vulnerable human form. God chooses to share our location and condition. *God is with us*. In the death of Jesus, we see God present in suffering human form. God chooses to take our part instead of being our enemy. *God is for us*. In the resurrection and ascension, we see God in victorious human form. In this form, insinuating himself into the depths of our very being, *God is in us*—as the Spirit of Christ. Three views of Jesus, three views of God.

Here, then, in a cameo, is the glory of God. Here is what God is really like. He is the God who is with us, the God who is for us, and the God who is in us. In short, when God shows his face, he always shows his grace; the treasure that he offers to lodge with us is nothing other than the grace of God. For when we say grace, we mean precisely this: the promise of God-with-us, the power of God-in-us, and the pardon of God-for-us.

Now we are ready for the major thesis. God now puts this treasure in earthen vessels, like us. Common clods of clay we are, and God invests his gift to humankind with us. Having once shown himself in Jesus, he shows his face now through our own ordinary humanity. Thereby hangs a miracle worth lingering over.

We have a figure of speech on our hands, of course. We are not really lumps of clay, we are magnificent human beings, the image of a beautiful God. But there are some things about us all that are like a lump of clay—enough, anyway, to give us a metaphor that says a lot about us and about how God comes on through people like us.

We should remind ourselves, first, that every

earthen vessel is unique, and that being an earthen vessel of God does not stereotype any one of us. Endless are the shapes that skilled hands at a potter's wheel can give to lumps of clay. Some are so plain you want to wrap them in macrame cords before you set them on your patio. But a pot of clay can be so exquisite that a John Keats will write an immortal poem to it. There is no single form, no single style, no single gender, no single color in earthen vessels.

But, endless in variety, earthen vessels still have some things in common; so do you and I, and we all have something in common with earthen vessels. I should like to suggest three properties of earthen vessels, properties that you have as well. Earthen vessels are *fragile*. Earthen vessels are *fallible*. Earthen vessels are *functional*. Let us see if you can find something of yourself in these qualities. And, maybe, find the face of God when you find yourself.

AN EARTHEN VESSEL IS FRAGILE

The finest pieces are sensitive, easily chipped, breakable. God did not put his treasure in a crushproof box, or a solid lead vault, or wrap it in styrofoam padding. He did not put his treasure with angels who never stub their toes or plastic saints you could drop from the Eiffel Tower without breaking them. Fragile earthen vessels he wanted. But this makes for pain and injury. You put clay pots next to each other, move them around, dust them off, let them get too close, and you will see damaged vessels—a cracked lip, a broken handle, a shattered vase. Mark this well, and take stock: if you agree to carry the treasure of God around, in the company of other earthen vessels, you are likely to become a cracked pot before you are finished.

You can get hurt in this business. Your soul can feel torn in two sometimes. There is conflict within you; you want to be a Christian in your heart, but you feel like the devil at the same time. There is conflict around you; you believe that God is good, but you cannot stomach the evil he seems to put up with in his world. It isn't easy to be the face of God when you know you are common clay. But you feel fragile, too, when other cracked pots get too close. They can hurt you, and knock you around inside, because they too are only earthen vessels. Remember, you are not the only lump of clotted clay around here. Fragility. It means easily damaged, frail, sensitive, not tough, breakable: do you fit the description? If you do, you can be reassured by St. Paul: the Almighty God invests his treasure in earthen vessels, and shows his face through fragile humanity like yours.

EARTHEN VESSELS ARE FALLIBLE

There is never a guarantee that an earthen vessel will succeed at the job for which you want it. Not every vessel is up to a perfect performance every time. A shallow pot will fail you if you want it to hold a plant with deep roots. A thin one will shatter if you try to pack it too tight. You cannot tell for sure by looking at it. So God takes a risk with earthen vessels; it's always a gamble when you have a high priority job and only ordinary servants to do it. And we take a risk with God, too; for it is hazardous to venture out as the bearer of God's grace when you know you could fall flat on your face.

Not long ago, I was asked to perform a task that I thought was quite an honor to be asked to do, and I took it on with cocky confidence that I could do it well. I did it, gave it what I thought was my best effort. I was not a success. I failed. I tried to find a more self-serving word for what happened; I tried to explain what happened by saying that they were not ready for me yet. But it did not work. The only explanation was: I tried it and I failed. I am better at being modest in my successes than I am at being graceful in my failures, so I did not take it well. I fretted about it; I had let people down and I didn't look too good myself. I did not deserve to be a grace-bearer for God. And then God came and seemed to say to me: You can take your choice. You can grovel before the gargoyles of your gothic pride, or you can adjust to my method. My method is to trust my treasure in earthen vessels, and to show my face through fallible humanity.

I dare say that there are a few nettlesome memories of failure that keep rattling in the closet of your mind. Maybe failures at your job, failures as a parent, failures as a moral person, and assorted others. If everyone knew you the way you know you, they might just wonder at God's sanity in gambling with earthen vessels like you. There is a line in Francis Thompson's *Hound of Heaven* that echoes how we sometimes feel about ourselves. Thompson had run away from God, fled him until God caught him. And God said what Thompson felt: "Of all earth's clotted clay, the dingiest clot; whom wilt thou find to love ignoble thee save me, save only me." Maybe you have felt that way—the dingiest clot of clay. If you have felt the sting of failure as an earthen vessel, hear this: God will never say that you are too dingy for his service, too grubby for his purpose, too common for his uncommon treasure. God puts his treasure in *fallible* earthen vessels, and no other.

EARTHEN VESSELS ARE FUNCTIONAL

Most clay jars are made to be of some use. I go to a museum and wonder about those vases that have survived the furies of volcanoes and tides of time; what were they for? The potter in his shop in a back alley of Athens three thousand years ago was not making a vase to be a collector's item to reveal the glories of Greek culture to museum buffs of the twentieth century. He was making a jar for a slave to carry water to his master's garden, or maybe a jug for wine to be served at a wedding. Most of the time, an earthen vessel is functional. It becomes a piece of art as a secondary matter. It is made mostly to carry and pour whatever someone puts in it. Earthen vessels of God function as pourers out of what God fills in. What God fills them with is himself.

Earthen vessels must be fillable in order to be functional. Somehow, in his subtle way, he has to get inside us; he has to come with his spirit, work his way into our consciousness, and become God in us. The God who is with us and for us becomes the God who is in us . . . and when he is in us, we become the functional vessels that share the treasure of his grace with other people. He does not force us; he invites us to open our lives to him, letting him gently and respectfully flow into our inner selves. If we refuse to let him work his way inside of us, if we are not fillable, we will not be functional. We may be ornamental, but he does not invest his treasure in bookshelf ornaments. *Fragile*, we are, and *fallible*, but *fillable and functional* we can be, earthen vessels containing God's finest gift.

God makes no apologies for how he shows his face to the human race. It is not as if he wanted something better, but has to put up with the likes of us. Earthen vessels are God's first choice. We are his kind of people for this job; he could have chosen the angel Gabriel, I suppose, but we were his type. If you ever get the notion that God only strings along with us until an angel comes along, you have not gotten the knack of God's style. God looked at the holy angels of the heavenly host and said: "You are not qualified; I need a fragile, fallible, functional, fillable earthen vessel." Cracked pots that we are, we are God's choice.

I sometimes think that God's choice of earthen vessels is the hardest thing about him to believe. People have always wanted God to use the superman scenario. They expected it when they met Jesus. "Walk upon my swimming pool," demanded the supercilious Herod in *Jesus Christ Superstar*.

God of glory in this clump of common Nazareth clay? No way; give us a superstar.

The earliest heresy in the Christian church happened when people denied that Jesus was a real human being. The same heresy gets into our heads when we hear that God might show his grace through our faces. We like to suppose that if we *really did* have God's treasure in us, we would be able to fly, swoop in from anywhere to rescue our children, rescue our friends, and win the heart of any Lois Lane. Fumbling old Clark Kents that most of us are, we bleed, we hurt, we can hardly cope, let alone rescue a threatened city. It is hard to believe—but God's way is to put his treasure in the Clark Kents of the world and not in supermen. So stop dreaming; you aren't going to be Superman, you're just an earthen vessel. But you are God's kind of clay pot.

Why does God do it this way? Why does he not use the star system, with all the ballyhoo and humbug of Hollywood hype? Or why does he not turn us into bionic women or six million dollar men overnight when he converts us? The answer is simple. Using earthen vessels is his way of keeping us alive to what is really going on. He wants to make it perfectly clear that when he uses us, it is his power and not our technique that does the job. God wants to keep us ready for surprises.

I recall the first time that someone came to me after hearing me preach a sermon to tell me that his life was affected and changed by what he had heard. God had gotten inside of him and turned some words of mine into bearers of pardon, of power, and of promise in his life. My first response was: Well, what do you know, it really works! And through me? Yes, even through me. And I think I have never gotten over the surprise. I have always felt in tune with what a recent convert to Christianity told everyone he knew. He had been a tough night-club operator at the time of his conversion, and did not think of himself as a prime candidate for God's service. So he witnessed to others by saying, "Look, buddy, if God could do it to me, you are a lead pipe cinch."

So with all of us. With God, we are a cinch, even though our clotted clay is not the stuff supermen are made of. Someone may just come up to you and say, "Your kind words encouraged me when I was in the pits." And you will know: the power was of God, but it came through me. Someone might say, "I was held back from doing a stupid, sinful thing because you had the courage to say no." And you can say: the power was of God, but thank God, he can do it through me. And if anyone ever experiences the helping grace of God in Jesus Christ through you, because of what you say or how you keep quiet and listen, you can know: he can use a common clod like me.

So, keep in touch with yourself as the fragile, fallible, but functional and fillable piece of ordinary humanity that you are. Keep in touch with yourself because, just as you are, you are qualified to hold and to share the treasure of God. Walk into the unknown possibilities of tomorrow with your human weakness, carry with you the blemishes of your soul and the commonness of your spirit. Just be the earthen vessel that you are. Let God fill you, and then you may be the hand and the heart, as well as the face of God, to someone who needs him more than he needs anything else in the world. When it happens to you, you will know for sure that no matter how wrong everything around you is, there is something most magnificently right with you.

8. If You Just Can't Cope, You Are Ripe for God's Opening Move

⦿§ THE GIFT OF AN OPEN HEART

. . . Pray for us also, that God may open a door . . . to declare the mystery of Christ . . .

Col. 4:3, RSV

I was just about to bend my six-foot-four frame into our eggshell blue 1952 Plymouth, to drive to a little church in the decayed center of Patterson, New Jersey. I was going to be ordained into the Christian ministry, a passage for which I felt tremblingly unprepared. Before getting into the car, I turned to my friend and former seminary teacher George Stob, who was standing by, and asked him: "George, do you have one last good word for me before I take this plunge?" George shot his answer back, as if it were long coiled tight in his mind, the one thing he thought I still needed to know. "Remember," he said, "that when you preach, you will be preaching to ordinary people."

Thanks a lot, I thought. For this kind of wisdom you get to be a professor in a theological seminary? As if I didn't know! Anyway, I stuffed his bromide into the bulging bag of expendable data I had garnered from seminary teachers and drove off to be ordained as a minister of the Gospel.

As it turned out, though, in my early years of arrogant innocence, I did not really know much about ordinary people. I did not know then, not in the depths of my being, not where the issues of a preacher's authentic attitudes are decided. I was ripe with scholarly insights. I was tuned in to my theology. I was tuned in to the craft of sermonizing. But I was not tuned in to the ordinariness of the people who listened to my idealistic preaching.

The poignant, painful book and film *Ordinary People* gave many of us a new definition of human ordinariness. A perfectionist mother tried so hard to crowd her little cosmos into her complete control, but could not cope when the foundations of her life quaked at the death of her favorite son. He drowned, and her power to love drowned with him. A son, the brother who survived, could not cope with his guilt for being alive when his brighter, better brother was dead. A father could not cope with the unsettling fact that the two people closest to him were hanging alone, out of his reach. These are ordinary people. To be ordinary is to be too weak to cope with the terrible stuff that is too much for mere humanity. Ordinary people are non-heroes—not cowards, just not heroes, limited folk, afflicted with the malaise of too-muchness.

We ordinary people cannot fit our lives into pre-formed, styrofoam boxes. We cannot manage life as well as we would like, at least not in our secret places. We cannot get all the strings tied; it won't wrap up the way we want it. For us, survival is often the biggest success story we dare hope for. Ordinary people are people who live on the edge, just a step behind the line that separates us from those who fall apart at the seams. Ordinary people are the ones who cry for a sign, any old sign, that it might still be all right even when everything seems horribly wrong.

What George was trying to tell me was that a lot of people who would be looking to God for help through me would be ordinary in this sense: they would be living, not on the peak of success, but at the edge of failure; not on the pinnacle of triumph, but at the precipice of defeat. He did not mean that everyone who came to me would be a failure. What he meant was that many of them would *feel* like failures sometime in their lives. It took me too long to learn how right he was.

St. Paul knew how hard it was for ordinary people to believe that their lives can be all right in the teeth of situations in which they are sure, absolutely certain, that everything is all wrong. This is why he asked for prayers—so that he could get the mystery of Christ through the closed doors of ordinary people's hearts. I am sure that the door he wanted to get through was *this* door, the door we close to the good news that it can be all right even when everything is wrong. What other door could he have needed to get open? He did not need a door to Rome or Europe; access was pretty free everywhere in the empire for a Roman citizen like Paul. No, not the door to a city, no miracle was needed to get through city gates. What he needed a miracle for was to get through the closed door of ordinary people's lives.

It is a quirk in ordinary people that they keep the door closed to the gracious gift of being all right when everything is all wrong. Down at the bottom, where feelings get too fierce for us to face, down where we press our anger into knots too tight to untie, we shut the door and keep it locked until God's invisible hand silently spins off the combination and gets through the door of pain and tiredness with the reality of Christ's grace. Ordinary people are people who have to struggle to make it and, in the struggle, turn away the gift that can enable them, not merely to make it, but to be very glad for the gift of trying.

They came to my church on Sunday, ordinary people did, but I did not recognize them in the early days. I know now why I did not recognize them; I did not want them to be ordinary people. I wanted them to be harts panting for the water brooks of my sermons. I wanted them to be minds buzzing like souped-up computers digesting my great ideas. I wanted them to be souls on tip-toe dancing to the spectacular music of the Spirit. I wanted them to be spiritual athletes, shoulders strong to bear the burdens of global justice that my prophetic words laid on them. But while I was offering them the precious promises and walloping them with the heroic mandates of the Word of God, many of them were secretly praying, "O God, I don't think I can get through the week—HELP ME!" What they needed beside my words was a miracle so that the door in the wall of their private too-muchness would open to the mystery of Christ.

I have since come to see a weak streak of ordinariness in smiling Christians who seem to have life tied neatly together. Sometimes, as I sit in a pew and listen to a preacher calling the people to "let justice roll down like waters, and righteousness like a mighty stream" over the market places and council chambers of every village, or promise the abundant life of joy and peace in the Spirit, I look around. And the *dramatis personae,* the characters in the churchly scenario, look like this for me:

A man and woman, sitting board-straight, smiling on cue at every piece of funny piety, are hating each other for letting romance in their marriage collapse on a tiring treadmill of tasteless, but always tidy, tedium.

A widow, whispering her Amens to every promise of divine providence, is frightened to death because the unkillable beast of inflation is devouring her savings.

A father, the congregational model of parental firmness, is fuming in the suspicion of his own fatherly failure because he cannot stomach, much less understand, the furious antics of his slightly crazy son.

An attractive young woman in the front pew is absolutely paralyzed, sure she has breast cancer.

A middle-aged fellow who, with his new Mercedes, is an obvious Christian success story, is wondering when he will ever have the guts to tell his boss to take his lousy job and shove it.

A Paulinely submissive wife of one of the elders is terrified because she is being pushed to face up to her closet alcoholism.

Ordinary people, all of them, and there are a lot more where they came from. What they all have in common is a sense that everything is all wrong

114

where it matters to them most. What they desperately need is a miracle of faith to know that life at the center is all right.

Why? Why is it so hard for the good news to get inside, into our feelings, whence it needs to percolate to the surface? Why do we need a gift of grace?

I do not think we need a gift of grace because the truth is so hard to understand. It is a mystery, of course, no question about that. But the mystery of Christ is not a secret code that only the elite can unravel. The heart of the matter is as uncomplicated as a Rotary Club joke. Someone once asked—if the legend is true—the great Karl Barth what it all came down to, all those thick books of his on theology. Barth, teasing maybe, but still serious, said: "It comes to this, 'Jesus loves me, this I know.'" The mystery comes down to something just this simple. Deep, profound, amazing, but simple.

The mystery is that God was in Jesus Christ reconciling the world to himself. When Jesus lived as a man on our native soil, living as a person who gave his life for others, dying and living again, he was about the business of making it right for us at the core of life. He let it be known to all, once and for all, that when we are confronted by the God who made us and holds us in his hands, we are facing a God who loves us and wants our good.

He built a bridge over the great gap that separated us from a holy God; the bridge he built was the cross where he was crucified. Since the cross of Christ, God and the world are reconciled, friends again, with God bent on turning the world, and our lives in it, into a thing of beauty and justice and glory. At bottom, where our lives hang by a thread of God's good will, it is really all right. And it will be all right. Nothing, nothing at all, nothing on earth, nothing in heaven, nothing up front, nothing behind, nothing we can do or anyone can do to us, nothing can change this fact: God loves you and wills your good forever.

Why do ordinary people lock their doors to this muscular comfort, this sweet reality? We have a galaxy of excuses. If we nag at ourselves a while, we can admit to some of them, even if it hurts. I will expose two reasons for keeping my door closed. See if they match yours.

First, we do not want to feel reconciled to God because we will complicate our lives if we are reconciled to him. Something always changes when we believe that life, in spite of everything, is all right, and we dread the change. For instance, we do not want to accept forgiveness because if we feel forgiven we will let go of some prime anger we stew up against some lousy people who did us wrong. We do not want to feel loved because if we accept love we may have to open our lives to someone we want to keep at arm's length. We do not want the joy of discovering that life is all right because if we do we may have to give up the pleasure of bitching about it, and we are just too tight to make that sacrifice. We do not want to live in the hope that God is going to make the earth a splendid place of justice and love because, if we have hope for a new creation, we may feel pushed to help prepare the way by making the world a little better than it is now. Kierkegaard was right; we choose to lock the door

116

of our hearts because we *want* to live in the wretched doghouses of our life.

Second, ordinary people keep the doors closed to their hearts because they are too tired to open them. It is not only as if ordinary people are just too perfervidly wicked to let the light of grace into their lives. Sometimes they are just too pooped. Self-pity drains our energy. We can hurt so much that we have no spiritual push left in us. We feel stuck in a void, sucked down into an empty pit where nothing can make us feel that life is all right. If we cannot locate energy to accept grace for ourselves, we surely cannot feel it for others; not because we are evil, but because we are exhausted.

As I think about being too tired to open our hearts' doors to divine grace, my thoughts are seduced back to my family's first two weeks in our present home. A dozen years ago, my wife and I and our three young children moved here, to California, from Michigan. We managed the first few days to get the kids into three separate schools. I started teaching a course at Fuller Theological Seminary I had never taught before, teaching it to 125 students at eight o'clock, four mornings a week. So far so good. After one week we learned from the hematologists at the City of Hope that our youngest son, just turned five, had Gaucher's disease, a rare congenital blood problem with an uncertain prognosis. A week later, two weeks after our arrival in the sun belt, we learned that my wife, Doris, had breast cancer and needed a mastectomy. Those were the first two weeks of our new life in the paradise of Southern California.

I remember getting home from the hospital one night after a visit with Doris, too tired to prepare for the next morning's lecture. I flopped on the bed and opened a copy of *Life* magazine, still coming out every Friday in those days. I paged lazily through it until I came to a section featuring the Nigerian civil war. Pictures of starving Biafran children, skin and bones, bulging empty bellies, knees like hard balls with toothpicks for legs sticking out of them. All the media at the time were throwing these pictures at our almost shock-proof consciences. But I shut the magazine tight. I threw it to the floor. I could not look. "I'm sorry, starving children, I am so tired; I need all my pity for myself tonight; I do not have energy to open my heart to compassion for you." I do believe it would have taken a miracle for me to get the door of my heart open to feel the love of a reconciling Christ for those Biafran kids that night. And it took another miracle to get me to *feel*, to deeply, truly, gladly *feel* that it was all right with me when everything, everything seemed all wrong. I was too tired to feel it by myself.

Ordinary people feel too tired a lot. They come to church and listen to words about a grace that has made life all right at the core. But they are often so muzzled by self-pity, so shackled by anger, and so paralyzed by their own real hurts that they cannot find the extra reserve of power to open their hearts to the reality of Jesus Christ and the fact of his grace. God needs to open the door.

The surprise is that God does give us the gift. Sometimes. And sometimes we accept it.

Sometimes people are sure that everything is all

wrong and they are tired of trying to make it right. Then God comes quietly to tell them that he is around them, above them, under them, in them, and ahead of them, and that with this surrounding shield of strong love, they are going to be all right.

Sometimes people are in the grip of anger that chokes their hearts, stifles their joy, and smothers every intimate relationship. Then God comes in to break the chain of anger and liberate an ordinary person for a new try at love.

Sometimes people live in quiet terror of their own death. Then God comes in to give them a reason for being very glad to be alive just for today.

Sometimes people brood over a depressing memory of some rotten thing they did and cannot forget nor forgive themselves for. Then God comes in to open their hearts to receive the gifts of other ordinary people's forgiveness and so come to forgive themselves.

Sometimes ordinary people wrap themselves like mummies in the suffocating sackcloth of their own self-hatred; and God comes to open their eyes to the extraordinary wonder of their great worth.

All ordinary people have a penchant for sensing that things are in insufferable shape around them. And they often are. Life can be miserable, horrible beyond enduring, the pits. But the secret of grace is that it can be all right at the center even when it is all wrong on the edges. For at the center, where life is open to the Creator and Savior God, we are held, led, loved, cared for, and inseparably bound into the future that he has for every child whom he claims as his. We cannot manipulate grace; I hope by this time I have made the point that grace is wondrously free. He gives it; we can only let him give it to us.

It took me too long to learn how much I needed George Stob's word about ordinary people. I should have known it a lot earlier. After all, I was one of them. No matter now. The important thing is that an extraordinary gift is available to ordinary people. It is the gift of an open door, the rusty hinged door of angry, hurting, and tired hearts, an open door for a grace that restores us to truth, the truth that, at the depths, between ordinary people and God, it is all right and always will be.

9. When You See the Angels, You'll Know Why You Believe

✑ THE GIFT OF FAITH ✐

Truly, truly, I say to you, you will see heaven opened, and the angels of God ascending and descending upon the Son of man.

John 1:51

I want you now to ask yourself one of the toughest questions that you can ask about your religious faith. The question is: why do you believe? Why do you trust in a God you cannot see? What keeps you coming back to your faith, in spite of your doubts and sometimes in spite of your pain? Surely you have wondered whether it really makes sense to believe there is a good God in heaven when things on earth around you are horrendous. There is, I think, a stubborn unbeliever inside every one of us. We all need to say, with the man who asked Jesus to heal his little boy: "Lord, I believe, help thou my unbelief." Sometimes we believe in spite of evidence that everything is so wrong that God must be dead. What is it, then, that keeps bringing us back to faith? What is the real reason we have for believing?

There is a scene in the New Testament where

Jesus talks to Nathanael, a skeptic soon to turn into a disciple, about reasons for believing (John 1:43–51). What he tells Nathanael brings us back to the beginnings, to the first grade of faith, and to the real reason for believing in God. We learn that the deepest reason for believing in God is nothing other than our experience of the grace of God. There, I have let the cat out of the bag. But come along with me, and see how Jesus gets the point across to a new disciple.

We have two conversations. One of them is between Phillip and Nathanael. In this conversation we hear Nathanael's wrong-headed reasons for not believing. The other conversation is between Jesus and Nathanael. In this conversation we hear Nathanael's muddle-headed reason for believing. Jesus is willing to accept him, muddle-headed or clear. But he knows Nathanael will discover a better reason for believing later on.

Let us play the tape again, slowly.

Scene One: Phillip and Nathanael.

Phillip has met Jesus. What a meeting! I do not mean that he had a chance to shake hands with the Master in a reception line, "Glad to see you, what was the name again?" Phillip had a deep encounter; he was grabbed by the mystery and authority in Jesus, and afterward nothing would ever be the same for him again. He felt divinity in Jesus' imperious command, "Follow me!" He knew, on the spot, that he had met the one whom all Israel was waiting for. I am sure he understood very little; he did not have to understand, he somehow believed, and in his faith he was ready to leave everything familiar to him and walk into the totally unfamiliar world of Jesus Christ.

Like anyone who has just had a life-changing meeting, he was burning to tell someone. So he ran to Nathanael. Listen, Nathanael, listen to me; we have met him, we have seen him, we know who he is, the One we've been waiting for to save us. His name is Jesus. He comes from Nazareth.

Nathanael probably thought Phillip had been brainwashed, or maybe he was joking. "Oh, of course, you just met the Messiah. I suppose he is a little green man with antennae coming out of his head. From Nazareth? Come, Phillip, we Jews do not play games about the Messiah. From Nazareth, indeed. Nothing good can come out of that town."

Nathanael was a skeptic. I think I can sympathize with him. After all, he had not met Jesus, had not heard him or felt him. All he had was a second-hand report. And goodness knows, what he heard was not what any Jew was conditioned to expect about the Messiah.

Suppose that someone came to you with the word that he had just met a young man who has all the answers to the world problems. He has the answer to the nuclear arms race, to inflation, to world hunger, to the energy shortage, and smog to boot. He is a young man just up from Tijuana, on welfare at the moment, and doesn't handle English too well as yet, but this is the man of the hour for the nations of the world. Would you not have just a slight temptation to say, "Can anything good come out of Tijuana?" You can understand Nathanael's skepticism.

No bookie in Las Vegas would have given Nazareth 10,000 to 1 odds. And why should the odds surprise us? The Gospel never suggests that Jesus Christ is what the betting public expected him to be. He upset almost everyone's notion of what a regular sort of Messiah would be like. The natural mind was not likely to fantasize the way it finally went when it actually happened. The *New York Times,* on hearing of it, would not have considered it news fit to print—the event too odd, the sources too suspect. An ordinary middle-class person, born in a nothing village in one of the grubbiest of all Roman provinces, claiming to be the Messiah—of course, the story is improbable.

But then everything about Jesus was highly improbable. You don't expect a carpenter's boy from Nazareth to grow up and give all humanity a new hope, you don't expect him to make us the children of God by dying on a cross. All told, I think, Nathanael's doubts were reasonable doubts; irrelevant in the end, of course, but reasonable under the circumstances.

I think Phillip sensed that Nathanael had a point. For he does not argue with Nathanael. He does not make a case for Nazareth; he does not say, "Well, Nazareth is a decent, religious little town," or whatever. Instead he has the only practical answer that believers can ever give a skeptic: "Come and see for yourself. Let me show you what I have seen. Try it, and be your own judge." This is the final defense of the Gospel, one that makes anyone a witness and one that disarms any skeptic. "I felt something in his presence, and I invite you to see for yourself."

So Phillip takes Nathanael to Jesus, and leads us into the second conversation.

Scene Two: Jesus and Nathanael.

Jesus watches Nathanael as he approaches, and greets the skeptic with a compliment. "Well, now here is an honest-to-goodness man of Israel." Now that was the finest thing anyone could say to an ancient Jew. What it came down to was something like this: "You are an honest Jew; no guile here, you are not a fake, you are an Israelite to the core of your being."

Nathanael is still skeptical; no one is going to sell him anything with such flattery. So he says: "How do you know what I am? You don't even know me." Again, a reasonable skepticism!

Jesus attacks his skepticism on its home grounds. "I do know you, Nathanael, I know you quite well. I knew you before you came. I knew you before Phillip got to you. I know the real you."

Nathanael is stunned. His skepticism melts like a snowball in Death Valley. That does it. This is a miracle. "I believe," he shouted, "I believe! You are the Son of God. A miracle like this is proof enough for me."

Well, that was quick. Nathanael's skepticism is blown away by one slight show of divine ESP. There was no sleeping on it. No consultation with theologians in Jerusalem. No FBI check on the man from Nazareth. No struggle. Instant conversion, from skeptic to believer in ten seconds. One sniff of a miracle, and Nathanael has his reason for believing.

Nathanael's faith is real enough for Jesus. Faith is faith, after all. Even if you do not have the most convincing reason for believing, you can still believe; and your faith can be a power for the rebirth of your life. Jesus does not question Nathanael's faith at all. He knows that Nathanael has a reason for believing, which he still was to discover. He has grabbed hold of the first reason that came along, and this is real enough for the time being. He has an explanation that makes sense to him now. But one day he would actually experience the real reason.

What is happening to Nathanael happens to us all, I suppose. We do things for reasons that we consider very sound at the time, only to discover later that our real reason for doing them went a lot deeper than we realized. I lost my temper with my wife. Mean show! I thought I was angry because she misplaced some papers. A night's sleep, a little thought, and I realized that I was really using my wife as a release for the anger I had bottled up against my boss. "Aha! Now I understand my real reasons for doing such a stupid thing." We all say it to ourselves, one time or another. Half of our struggle in growing up is coming to terms with the *real reasons* we have (and often hide) for doing the things we do. The same is true in our spiritual growth. It takes time and it takes growth to uncover the real reason we have, even for the basics—being a believer, for instance. Our hearts have reasons our heads are too superficial to know—at first.

Jesus understood this about Nathanael. One day, he said, later on, further down the avenue of your experience, you will learn the real reason for believing in me. You have a reason—this miracle you think you saw. But there is something deeper. And this is how it will come to you: "You will see the heavens opened up and angels coming down upon and going up from the Son of Man." When you see the angels, you will know the real reason you believe.

Now, as you may recall, Jesus is alluding to Jacob and to Jacob's famous ladder. Remember the story? Jacob was running hard across the desert from the brother he had tricked out of an inheritance. But while escaping a brother, he was caught by God. Jacob had an experience with the grace of God at a desert waterhole called Peniel, and came out of it a changed man. On that occasion he had a dream; he saw a ladder pitched between earth and heaven, with angels climbing up and clambering down to earth again. It was only a dream, so we should not worry about whether heaven is really "up" or why angels would need a ladder. The ladder was a sign that Jacob could be right with God only because God descended from heaven to meet him on earth. So Jesus tells Nathanael that he would know what his real reason for believing was when he had an experience like Jacob's—the experience of being conquered by the grace of God.

Let's focus on the point again. The point is that there are many reasons for believing, but only one real reason. There are many reasons of the head, but the one real reason lies in the heart. Take a poll of believers. Ask them why they believe. You will find almost as many reasons as you find believers. But at bottom, they all share one real reason.

Let me tell you some reasons why I believe. I think every one of them is genuine. I know none of them is enough.

MY FAMILY

I believe because I was brought up in a believing family. I make no bones about it. I don't know what would have come of me had I been born in a Manchurian family deep in China. But, as it was, I was led to believe in God as soon as I was told to eat my oatmeal. We did a lot of believing; we had to because faith was about all we had. Other kids sang: Jesus loves me, this I know, for the Bible tells me so. I might have sung: Jesus loves me, this I know, for my mother told me so. I am not alone. A reporter once asked the great theologian Karl Barth: "Sir, you have written many huge volumes about God; tell me, how do you know it is all true?" The learned German, eyes laughing, is said to have answered, "My mother told me."

Families are God's primary missionary societies. His romance with the human race is a family affair. We believe often enough because our parents first told us about the love of God and then lived the love in front of us.

But it does not always work this way. Some children become unbelievers because of their families. They quit believing that a heavenly father loves them because their earthly father never did. And, besides, a lot of people become Christians in spite of the unbelief of their parents. Our families may be a help, but they are never the real reason for believing.

THE CHURCH

I believe because the church put its arms of caring ministry around me and, sometimes, put the fear of God inside me. My faith was conceived in the womb of the Body of Christ. St. Augustine may have exaggerated some when he said, "I would never have believed had it not been for the church." But it was the church, after all, that parlayed the message of Jesus across the ages; the church has seen to the translation of the Scriptures, the enlisting of missionaries, and the preaching of the Gospel to every new generation. I know the church is an earthen vessel, and sometimes it seems that the Gospel is likely to be true if only because any notion that could survive the bungling of the church must be true. But, for all its humanity, the church is still Jesus' way of walking the streets and alleys of every ancient and every modern town. The church gets credit for an assist when people believe.

But it is not the real reason. The church is, in fact, often a very serious stumbling block to faith. Some people feel just the opposite of St. Augustine; they say, "I might believe if it were not for the church." When people get a shocking peek at the seamy, sin-infected side of the fallible church, they often become cynics instead of believers. The church cannot be the real reason for believing; there must be something deeper.

THE ARGUMENTS

Then there are all those arguments to prove that God exists and to prove that Jesus is who he said he was. Perhaps you have listened to them. I think I have heard them all. Some of them, frankly, could not stand up under a good counter-attack. But many of the arguments are helpful for me. Some of them are really persuasive. I, for one, am helped a good deal by sound arguments that Jesus really must have risen from the dead. Good arguments can be a real support in our believing, and even poor ones help the people who are convinced by them.

But they cannot be the real reason, not for me at any rate. If I rested my faith on my ability to prove it, I would always wonder whether some smart young philosopher would come along with a better argument against believing than I had for believing. Besides, there are a lot of questions I still cannot answer. I cannot give a convincing answer to why some people have to suffer as much as they do. A little suffering, yes, I can understand that, but I do not understand why innocent children have to suffer so much sometimes. No, I cannot rest my faith on my arguments; I cannot rest with my ability to think things through. The real reason for believing must come from another corner of my life.

THE BIBLE

"The B-I-B-L-E, yes that's enough for me. I stand alone on the Word of God—the B-I-B-L-E." We sang it, all us kids in Bible school sang it as our epistemological premise. Only the Book, and the Book is enough! The book tells us of Jesus. The book teaches us of grace. The book tells us what to believe. Christian faith is heir to the book, it feeds from the book, it is taught by the book. Only the people who keep listening to the word keep faith alive. The church that turns away from the book is bound to be a loser, as far as faith is concerned. The Bible is solid reason for believing in Jesus Christ.

But it is not the real reason. It is a necessary, but not a sufficient reason. I do not believe in Jesus because I first believed in the Bible. I believe the Bible because I first believed in Jesus. I met Jesus in the Scriptures, and I knew that the book that tells me about the love of God in Jesus must be true. Jesus is the really real reason for believing the Bible, not the other way around.

Well, what have I left? If it is not my family, not my church, not my arguments, and not even the Bible, what is the real reason for believing? Why do I believe?

Let's get back to the text. Jesus said to Nathanael, "You will see the angels coming down from heaven upon the son of Man, and when you see them you will know the really real reason you believe in me."

Once again, the angels are a flashback to Jacob, the crooked wheeler-dealer in whom guile flowed like water down Niagara Falls. The man with the fast pitch who had cheated his brother out of his inheritance by a "sleight of arm" trick. Now he was running, running from his brother, running from his God. A fugitive from a gracious God? Jacob had no chance. For God had a mind to catch him. He fled, but God outmaneuvered and out-persisted him, and eventually caught him. When he was caught by God, he discovered that he had been subdued by grace.

Francis Thompson, that poor, sad, Christian

poet, probably had Jacob in mind, as well as him-self—and us—when he wrote "The Hound of Heaven" about his own flight from grace.

I fled him, down the night and down the days;
I fled him, down the arches of the years;
I fled him, down the labyrinthine ways
Of my own mind; and in the mist of tears
I hid from him . . .
From those strong feet that followed, followed
   after.

But with unhurrying chase,
And unperturbed pace,
Deliberate speed, majestic instancy,
They beat—and a voice beat
More instant than the feet—

That voice is round me like a bursting sea . . .
Lo, all things fly thee, for thou fliest me.

Whom wilt thou find to love ignoble thee
Save me, save only me . . .

Ah fondest, blindest, weakest,
I am he whom thou seekest . . .

This is what Jacob discovered. He was running away from the source of love, running away from grace. But he could not escape. God is too persistent in his love, too stubborn in his grace. And, when he was caught, he discovered that the one chasing him was not his enemy, but his best friend.

This was the meaning of Jacob's dream. His

ladder said that heaven was coming to earth and that heaven could be reached from earth; the angels coming down the ladder meant that God was reaching down for sorry earth and sinful people. The blessing of heaven was coming down to earth and earth's sorrows could be carried up again to heaven. The line between heaven and earth was open. The vision of the angels was the vision of the grace of God coming into human life.

Jesus told Nathanael that he, like Jacob, would see the angels. But there is no hint in the Bible that he or any other disciple ever saw literal angels, not climbing down a ladder at any rate. Jesus was not talking about what a person sees with his physical eyes. Jesus meant that Nathanael would come to see that his real reason for believing was the same as Jacob's reason—an experience with God the hunter, the hunter who chases, chases, until he captures, captures his human prey with love, and holds him with grace.

So it is, with us still, the deepest reason for our believing is that we have seen Jacob's ladder, not at Peniel in the ancient desert, not in Judea, but in Los Angeles, or in Chicago, Moscow, or Sioux Center.

Enter Francis Thompson again, with words from "In No Strange Land." Poor poet that he was, he slept under the sky on the banks of the river Thames. He earned pennies to survive by holding horses for people while they shopped at Charing Cross. A wretched lot for a great poet! But he wrote for everyone who, like himself, was bent by the unfairness of life, saddened by the suffering, and

133

puzzled by the heavy-handed wrongness of so much of life.

> But, when so sad thou canst not sadder,
> Cry—and upon thy so sore loss,
> Shall shine the traffic of Jacob's ladder
> Pitched betwixt Heaven and Charing Cross.

> And lo, Christ walking on the water,
> Not of Gennesaret, but Thames.

Do you begin to feel the message Jesus had for Nathanael? And for us? The really real reason we keep believing, in the midst of our sadness, and in spite of our doubts, is that we have seen "the traffic of Jacob's ladder, pitched between heaven and the place of our troubles." We have known the grace of God pulling us back when we felt like running away.

The conclusion of the matter is this: I have seen the angels on Jacob's ladder, and this is why I believe. I do not believe because I was reared in a believing family. I do not believe because the church got to me early enough. I do not believe because I first was persuaded that the Bible is true. And I do not believe because I have thought it all through on my own.

I believe because God's grace grabbed me and grabs me still in the deepest depths of my life, and will not let me go. He keeps coming after me, and when I most want to leave him he subdues me by his love. He will not let me stop believing. When I find myself believing him, I know it must be all right with us even when things are sadly, shabbily, stupidly wrong.

He comes with a pungent taste of pardon when I go wrong, comes with a quiet nudge of power when I feel helpless, comes with a subtle hint of hope when I lose courage. When he comes, he gives me, each time new, the real reason why I believe and cannot stop believing. He supplied the reason when he opened heaven, put a ladder down to earth, and came with grace to me. I cannot stop believing even when my head tells me that too many things are wrong in my world for God to be true. For when I feel the triumph of grace in my beleaguered soul, I know that, at bottom, it is all right, and will be all right everywhere before God is through with me.

10. God Takes His Time, So Why Not Take Yours?

❧ THE GIFT OF PATIENCE ❧

And should not I pity Nineveh, that great city . . . ?
Jon. 4:11, RSV

This is a story about God's compassion and a man's righteous anger, and the classic struggle between them. God plays himself, the patient One; Jonah is his impatient prophet. The conflict erupts over the question of God's Nineveh policy. Should God take the hard line against the godless, atheistic, and violent Nineveh? Should he use his first-strike capability and smash the violent city? Or should he wait, hold back the divine holocaust, and give the city a chance? What will it be, a policy of gracious compassion or a policy of impatient indignation? I wonder whose side you are on.

Let us watch the Lord and his prophet square off against each other on the momentous issue of God's response to the violent city. There are two encounters in the story (Jon. 3, 4). First, God's encounter with the city itself. Second, God's encounter with Jonah. Here, God defends his Nineveh policy of compassionate patience against Jonah's first-strike indignation. Two scenes, then: God and the city, and God and the prophet.

GOD AND THE CITY

The city is Nineveh. It is a great city in the style of the ancient world. Like every city of every age, it is a mixture of curse and blessing, the worst and best of all possible worlds. It is the center of culture, it has the best schools, the best hospitals, the best theatre, the best music, the highest technology—a great place to live. Here also are the loneliest people, the craziest lifestyles, the most corrupt politics, the most blatant immoralities, and, above all, the worst violence—a terrible place to live.

In the Bible, the civilized city is a puzzle. On the one hand, the city is the godless place; if you want to find God, you have got to hike to the mountains or trek into the desert. God is at the edge of a trout stream, not in the smoke-filled rooms of city hall. And yet, when inspired fantasy projects the metropolis as God's own place, the center of his holy presence, his home, Jerusalem is the holy city, the city of God. So the city can be either place: ultimate Godforsaken Sodom or ultimate God-renewed Jerusalem.

Nineveh is the ultimate in cultured Godforsakenness. It is an atheistic cauldron of violence. God cannot stomach the violence; he cannot suffer humanity's dehumanizing brutality. We are not told what sort of violence infuriates him the most. Is it the violence of an economic system against the poor? Is it military violence? Or is it just the violence of the hoods and the thugs on the street? Maybe it's all of them lumped together, including the violence of some husbands against wives, making Nineveh the symbol of all violent civilization.

Jonah was as furious about Nineveh's violence as God was. So God sent the prophet to the city to announce that he, the Lord, was finished with it. The indignant prophet, with a spoonful of violence in his own self-righteous heart, goes to the task with lip-smacking relish. He had set out once before, you recall. But then he suspected that God would turn out to be a soft-hearted liberal in the crunch, and would cop out when the time came to push the red button. At that time, a whale came between him and Nineveh. Now he is there, preaching damnation with fire in his belly. He lets the city know what God is going to do: waste the city, wipe it out, burn it down. God is angry as heaven and he is not going to put up with it anymore. So, in forty days, thirty days plus ten, God will send his terrible swift sword and his fiery whirlwind against Nineveh. There is no way out. Nineveh will be finished.

Jonah proclaimed the message with a dry eye; no tears flowed down his cheeks as he predicted Nineveh's doom. They deserved it, they had it coming, these godless atheistic people of the East. And I guess he had a point. We do well to notice that God never argued with Jonah about Nineveh's faults; the Lord does not defend or excuse the violence of the city.

So Jonah proclaimed doom for thirty-nine days and then stepped aside to watch the mushroom cloud on the fortieth day. But the awful day came and nothing special happened. The sun rose, the kids went out to play little league, men went to work, and women did whatever women did in that ancient city. The dance of the city went on just as before. The holocaust had been postponed.

What happened? Two amazing things. One happened in the city. The other happened in God. The city changed. God changed. When both had changed, 120,000 human beings lived to see another day.

The city changed. This is perhaps the most incredible change of all. The great city of man, the wicked creation of sinful culture, was converted. It began with ordinary people; they repented of their violence. They saw how self-destructive and self-defeating it was for human beings to get their way by brutal assault against each other. They repented and put away violence. And their private conversion caught on; it spread from families, where husbands put away violence against their wives, to neighborhoods, to city hall, and finally to the royal palace itself. The king of Nineveh led the nation in a pageant of penance; a new royal policy against violence was issued. The city changed—not forever, not perfectly, not from top to bottom, but at least in heart; it determined before God to put away violence as the solution to conflict.

We must let this almost incredible fact sink in slowly. For it is a parable of what is possible in the city of man. Nineveh is a biblical symbol of the violence-prone civilization that the sinful genius of humanity has created. It stands for Washington, Moscow, Berlin, Peking, all the great centers of power, and their drift toward ultimate violence against the human race. The conversion of Nineveh

139

tells us that our civilization is not caught in an unbreakable grip of violence. Nor are we helpless captives in a train that is rushing headlong, unstoppable, toward nuclear disaster.

We can decide against violence. We can stop the nuclear arms race; we can call off the madness; we can step off the escalator that is rushing us toward the killing of ten million innocent children. Nineveh is a straw in the wind. The city of man can change at least this much: it can put away violence as the final solution to its problems.

If we do not believe the city can change, we do not believe in the presence and the power of God.

The second change was in God. God changed his mind. One day God said: Nineveh's clock has run out; its day of death has come. The next day God said: Let Nineveh live, let its clock run awhile longer, let women give birth to babies, let young men and young women dream dreams of the future, and let the dance of life continue. I am not sure whether God's change of mind comes as a surprise to you. To a Calvinist like me, a divine change of mind twists the nose of a long-standing theological bias. Does God really change his mind?

The answer is yes, God changes his mind. But he never changes his heart. There, in the depths of his compassionate heart, God is eternally unchangeable. The purpose of his heart is to seek and to save the lost, to heal the hurt, to reconcile the alienated, to liberate the captives, and to recreate the world to a Kingdom of Peace. He is not willing that any should perish; this is the unchanging intent of his great heart. And if he needs to change his mind, to shift his strategy, to alter his course, to achieve his heart's purpose, then he changes it. God is not the great stone face of heaven. "Thou changest not, thy compassions they fail not"—this is the line that expresses an authentic theology of the unchangeable God. God is unchangeable forever—in his compassion toward the city of men.

The two changes, the change in the city and the change in God, mean that the city of humanity is given time. The people are given breathing space. History goes on awhile. Let all who love life, let all who have an ounce of compassion in their souls give thanks.

GOD AND THE PROPHET

Not Jonah. Jonah is standing in the wings with egg all over his face. He is seething. Most of all, he is hopping mad at God. And he has two reasons for his anger.

First, he is furious because God made a fool out of him in front of the whole city. What a way to treat a prophet! You order him to proclaim to one and all that disaster is on its way; no loopholes, no escape clauses, no strings. The city will be destroyed on June 21, 981 B.C., or thereabouts. And what happens? Nothing, zero, thud. God made Jonah look like the fellow who promised his cult disciples they would all be raptured into the sky on June 21, A.D. 1981. Or like the prophets who told us that California would slide into the ocean in August 1969. This is no way to support the collapsible ego of an insecure preacher. So, Jonah is sore; God punctured his prophet's pride.

But his anger goes deeper. It has to do with the

141

kind of world we live in and the sort of God we have to live with. Jonah wants a world where the bad guys always get what is coming to them, and get it before the third act is over. He believes in the justice of the quick execution; answer violence with violence, give the devil his due at once.

When no cloud of destruction broke over Nineveh on the fortieth day, the moral seams of the universe came apart. Nothing less than the moral state of the universe was at stake. How could you ever trust God again to face up to his duties? How could you trust a God who lets compassion get the upper hand over moral judgment? How can you trust a God of grace to face up to evil in our world?

So what does a morally outraged prophet do when God's compassion turns back instant annihilation? He retires to the suburbs, that's what he does. He never liked the city anyway. He sets up a chaise lounge on his patio, mixes a drink, and waits. Give him some time and maybe God will get hold of himself again, grab some grit, send his terrible thunder eastward, strike the city, and destroy the enemy after all. Meanwhile, Jonah was going to quit the prophet game, get a little pleasure out of life. He stationed himself alongside the swimming pool while he waited to see whether the mushroom cloud would after all ascend over the ashes of the violent city.

Now comes the encounter between God and his prophet. God has to explain his new Nineveh policy to the man who has been his chief spokesman for the old policy. So, God visits Jonah at the side of his pool.

GOD SPEAKS FIRST: Jonah, I'm getting some bad vibrations from you. You're really uptight.

JONAH: After what you pulled on me, I'm outraged. I'm so hurt I wish I were dead.

GOD: You want to talk about it, Jonah?

JONAH: Yes, I want to talk about it. I knew you were soft at heart. I suspected you would get compassionate on me. I should have listened to my own instinct and stayed away from Nineveh as I did the first time.

GOD: But, Jonah, why be angry with me?

JONAH: [No answer.]

Well, if Jonah will not listen, maybe an object lesson will speak to him. Enter the vine! A magnificent vine grows up overnight and gives a tired prophet some beautiful shade while he takes his ease waiting for the showdown over Nineveh. What a vine! At last count some 239 doctoral dissertations have been devoted to discovering the botanical identity of that vine. But then the worm comes. A huge and hungry worm! With a giant crunch, the worm destroys the vine. Some worm!

Now Jonah is wild. Who wouldn't be? A hot wind is blowing, the sun is beating on his bald head, and his swimming pool is filled with refuse from the worm-eaten vine. I have blown my cool at lesser things. In any case, God has made his point. So he comes to Jonah again.

GOD: We have felt your rage all the way up in heaven, Jonah. Do you think it's therapeutic to get this angry?

JONAH: Oh, at least I know now exactly where I am with you, Lord. What it finally comes down to now is this: You force us to live in a rotten world supposedly run by a fuzzy-minded, soft-spined, liberal God. Well, the fact is, I don't want to live in this kind of world; I want out. I would rather die. Things are never going to be right again; God is soft on evil.

GOD: It was the vine that did it to you, wasn't it, Jonah? You feel something. You feel for that plant. You let that beautiful vine get to you. Well, if you can feel for a vine . . .

> should not I pity Nineveh, that great city, in which there are more than a hundred and twenty thousand persons who do not know their right hand from their left, and also much cattle?

Are we getting the picture? Jonah saw only wickedness; God saw people. Jonah saw the violent power structures; God saw weak people. Jonah saw the evil and was indignant; God saw people and was compassionate. Therein lay the conflict.

It lies there still. Morally indignant people have a compulsion to divide all people cleanly between friends and enemies, good guys and bad guys, and want instant judgment and execution for the enemies and bad guys. God sees the human race as people, all of whom are part good and part evil, and he is willing to give them all a chance, to let them have more time, to let the world go on awhile "because he is not willing that any should perish."

But the Jonahs of the world say, "They are so evil, so hopelessly evil." "Yes," God replies, "but consider the children. If you cannot have compassion for the Brezhnevs of the world, what about the little ones?" (No child ever asked to be born in Nineveh, or in Russia or China; no child ever earned the right to be born in the United States. No baby ever chose to be born in a coldwater flat in the heart of the city's ghetto.) "What about the children, Jonah? If you want the violent leaders to get what is coming to them, what do the little children have coming to them? When Nineveh goes up in flames, the children burn with it. Remember the children, oh, you Jonahs of the world."

And even the cattle. God has compassion even for the animal world. Why should he slaughter all the animals of Nineveh? Why not let the world go on in its petty pace for a little while longer?

What we see in God's way with Nineveh is a parable of God's way with human history, his way with sinful people, his way with us. It is the answer to the age-old question: Why does God let human history go on when everything seems so wrong in it? Why does he wait so long to burn it all up in the great conflagration of the ages? It is a parable of the truth expressed by the Apostle Peter in the New Testament. When people scoffed at the prophecy that Christ would return to judge the old world and recreate it into a new one, Peter explained why God took so long. "God is not willing that any should perish, but that all should come to repentance" (II Pet. 3:9).

Compassion moves God to put up with things awhile longer for the sake of people. God puts up with loose ends, with hardness of people's hearts, with worlds full of wrongness, always to give people a chance to come back to him. Compassion does not rush into judgment. It patiently waits for a new day, a tomorrow when things may change. Compassion is the power not to foreclose on the future.

We need a dose of God's compassion in our time. We must see more than the evil of the alien enemy. We need to see beyond the godless systems, the threatening philosophies of alien powers. We need to look through God's eyes and see the enemy as ordinary people. We need to bring the voice of the compassionate God to bear on the Pentagon and the Kremlin; we need to tell them violence is not an incurable habit and that atomic disaster is not our inescapable destiny.

For two thousand years the Christian eye has been focused on Jesus Christ as the final solution to human violence. The apostle Peter said it early on: "We wait for new heavens and a new earth in which righteousness dwells" (II Pet. 3:13, RSV). We have been looking ever since. We look to the day when we all beat our atomic weapons into plowshares, when we all learn war no more, when we all put away violence as the answer to our problems. If we can keep this long-range perspective, we will not demand immediate violent answers to our problems; we do not need to settle the score now, once and for all, at this moment. We know the final answer is coming in God's own time. So let us cool our rage against the enemy, let us hold back the hatred, restrain our indignation, and drink the spirit of patience from a compassionate God.

There will be enough people among us to demand first-strike power to destroy the enemy. There will be enough indignant and impatient prophets who believe that God wants America to be the agent of his wrath against the cities of the enemy. These are the Jonahs of our time. Let Christian people, who have learned compassion first-hand from the cross of Christ, talk of giving peace a chance, of delaying the day of disaster, and of letting the human race go on until Jesus comes.

God's compassionate patience is also the answer to our personal impatience. From the control center of our worried lives, God's patience often looks like cold indifference. He takes so awfully long that he does not seem to care. But he has a lot of time and, like an artist who loves his work, he will not be rushed. Nor should we be rushed, especially when it comes to closing down, terminating, giving up on the nasty problems we want solved now. We should not give up too quickly when everything goes wrong. We should not give up too quickly on our troubled marriage. We should not give up too quickly on our troubled children. We should not give up too quickly on our troubled selves. Don't demand that everything be all right today. Give God time, as he gives us time.

The conclusion of the matter is that God gives us grace to imitate his patience. He gives us a choice. Will we be the Jonahs of the world who demand instant and violent solutions to our problems? Or will we let God take his time, and let him show us, in his way, that we do not have to foreclose on the future, let him show us that it can get to be all right tomorrow even though everything seems incredibly wrong today. When he does, he will make it feel all right *with us* beginning today, even if we have to wait for the rest.

11. If You Fall into Hell, You May Land in the Hand of God

◆§ THE GIFT OF BEING HELD §◆

If I make my bed in hell . . . even there your right hand will hold me.

Ps. 139:8, 10

I was alone in a plain red cottage on Fox Island, not far out into Puget Sound, off the sober fishing town of Gig Harbor in the state of Washington. I stayed there a couple of years ago, for three weeks into Indian summer. I had no radio with me, no television, and no stereo—which meant having no ball games, no eleven o'clock news, and no Mozart before supper. I took no newspaper, had no magazines, and read no books. I did not smoke or drink wine, and I did not talk on the telephone. Twice a day, ten in the morning and four in the afternoon, I took myself for a walk down the gravel road in front of the cottage to the bay and along the bay to the bridge that tied us to Gig Harbor. Most mornings, early, I talked for a while with John Finch, my guide on this inner journey. For the rest, I kept inside the cottage to consult with my soul. In the middle of the second week, on a Wednesday afternoon, long about four o'clock, I felt the presence of God. I discovered the old Hebrew verse-maker was right: you can lie down in hell and find yourself in the hand of God.

Everything I have tried to say in this book up to now is false if this is not true: that we can feel God in our hells, beneath us, around us, to hold us up and hold us together when we are sinking into a bottomless pit of our own undoing. Everything is true if this is true: if we can find God in hell, we can find God anywhere. But in order to find him, we must feel him. The key is feeling: we will discover him, I dare say, only as we feel him.

I want to tell you how I felt God that warm afternoon on Fox Island, I want to tell you how that one hour's experience has become a parable, for me, of how we can know for sure, by experience, that it really can be all right, in the center of life, when everything on the surface is hellish.

Being alone, shorn of my assorted psychic crutches, was just a way of clearing the decks. Aloneness is no magic entrée to God; it is just a way of cleaning out the clutter that tends to clog the valves of deeper feelings. When I have no tv, I cannot run away in order to catch the Rams on Channel 2. When I have no book to read, I find it just a little harder to stifle feelings in a blanket of ideas. When I have no people to chatter with, it is a little harder for me to turn God off so I can gab with a friend. So I merely closed down a few of my routine escape routes. If I did not meet God, it was not to be because I fenced him off with the defenses of everyday diversions.

Hell, as anyone knows, is where you do not expect to find God. Hell is the ultimate in our feeling of going-wrongness. It is the last word in nothingness, quintessential Godforsakenness. So my experience ran against the grain of what I could reasonably expect. In fact, I do not think I could have felt him as I did unless I went to hell first and let him find me there.

I must trust you to understand me. You do not need to wait to die before you experience hell. We have our mini-hells, too, many of them planted, like the four-corner towns you find along Route 83 in southern Arkansas, at most any crossroad of our private pilgrimages. Mini-hells are as real as the absolute pit, only less final; they are the hells of our feelings, and it is just as amazing to feel God in them as in the big one down the pike. The point is: to feel yourself in God's hands in the pit of your personal hell is to know it is all right when everything is totally wrong.

But does it really happen? Is God himself—the real one—there, at the depths, in the hard place, where everything is wrong as hell? Was the old Hebrew only romanticizing when he expected God's hand to hold him up while he sank through the black hole of hades, slipping down the frozen excrement of hell, the no-man's land of the lost? I can only tell you that when I felt God, I really did feel *him;* I did not feel a feeling that felt like a feeling of God. I was nestled in the hands of God, strong fingers cupping me in the tactile grip of love. Do not expect me to argue the point. Do not expect me to calculate the odds, weigh the evidence for God in hell. You will just have to indulge me as I tell you what I felt.

We need, though, to be serious about those hands

150

of God. He does have hands. We should not play school and talk about figures of speech—metaphors and the like. God's hands are not metaphors. Our human hands are metaphors. When I do my handiwork, I am an apprentice at imitating God, a clumsy likeness at that. He lets us call our five-fingered extremities hands only because they are something like his hands. His are the real ones, the originals, the archetypally creative hands. This is why, when we are shoved into our mini-hells or when we make our own beds there, it is life and death whether his hands are really holding us or not. God's hands in hell are the primal security. You enter the eye of grace, the ultimate safety zone, when you feel, in hell's bed, God's own hands holding you up.

Have you noticed how much we need human hands to make things right for us, to keep us out of our mini-hells? Of course, you have. But do not think only of surgeon's hands that slice out your tumors, nor of a genetic engineer's hands that try to improve the human stock by shuffling the genes around inside our secret DNA. Think instead of your mother's hand patting you on the head, just heavily enough to tell you that your most important person thinks you are a good child, good enough for her to love you. Think of your friends slapping you hard over your shoulders, what a whacking you are willing to take to get a feeling of being one of the gang. Sometimes, if you are lucky, you may even get to have people smack their hands together for you so you can know how much they appreciate your performance. One whopping hand-clap is like Lourdes for a crippled ego. Then there is the soft stroke, the intimate brush, the sensuous caress of a hand barely touching your skin, a hand that signals caring, desire, acceptance—a wish for you to know that you are able to fill another's life with joy.

What are these hands to us? They are almost everything, they are the hands of our human gods, the hands that tell us we are all right, and that it is all right with us. They make us feel approved. They make us feel as if we are nice people, liked, wanted, admired. They are the hands that hold us and keep us from falling into the mini-hells of our deepest feelings. We can miss a few of them at a time, but we could not miss all of them, not all of them at once. If no hands touch us, none pat us, none stroke us, none applaud us, we are lost. Oh, God, how we need these human hands. If they leave us, we make our bed in hell.

A lot of us scurry through our lives scared to death that human hands will not reach out to where we are—that we will not feel their approving pats on our head. Maybe it is even worse to be left alone without stroking than to be told a surgeon's hands cannot take away our tumors; more hellish to be rejected than to be inoperable. I would not care to guess. But I do know it can be hell to be left dangling in the winds—no mother's milk of moral affirmation, no applause, no reinforcement, no support—only yourself. Only with what you are inside, only your own very being, with nothing beneath to keep you from falling down.

So—we are down to the bottom line. We make our beds in hell whenever human hands stop patting us on the head the way mother used to do, or when we realize, at last, that all the hands in the world cannot stroke us enough to make us sure it is all right. We flop in hell's bed when human hands fail us, one way or the other.

It happened to me on a sunny September Wednesday; I fell into my mini-hell and landed in the hands of the living God. I cannot provide details of the fall; twenty-five years of thinking and teaching about God's ways leave me with no verbal tools to do more than say how it felt to me. My savvy friends who know all about psychology will tell you I had an acute anxiety attack. Maybe they are right. I can only tell you that what I experienced was the saving presence of a loving God who put his hands under me when I was dangling, dry, hung out in nothingness where no human hand was able to reach out and hold me up.

I was pacing the short stretch of floor between a stuffy little living room and a gray area near the kitchen crowded with a square wood table and four wobbly chairs from Goodwill; you can find a mini-hell any old place. As I walked my petty pace, I got more and more nervous about the gap between the doctrine of grace computed into my Calvinist cerebral cortex and my secret fantasy of earning God's applause by being a fine Christian fellow. Down inside, where my boyhood survives, I needed somebody's pat on my head, somebody's stroking, somebody's clapping; I couldn't be sure of God's approval unless I got it from people around me.

I had, in fact, gotten mother confused with God; I needed her approval, when you came right down to it, as much as I needed God's. She became my stand-in God, and I feared it was as hard to get her approval as it was to get God's. Friends, too, and of course wife and colleagues, anyone with hands to

153

stroke me, I needed them all; they all became substitute mothers and substitute gods to justify my life.

For some people, the little boy or girl inside is the fun kid, the crazy, impulsive, playful little dickens hiding in the bulrushes of their sober adult souls. For me, the boy inside was just a rotten kid who knew he had to be something better than he was in order to get mother's, or God's—the two never got separated—approval. The boy inside me was a frightened little Pharisee, chasing the carrot of divine approval at the end of an endless stick. But my carrot took the shape of mother's own "well done thou good and faithful boy," and I never reached it, and could never reach it, not if I tried a million years.

So, what can you do, what can you do except knock yourself out chasing all those wonderful virtues, faking it too often, now and then downgrading yourself so you would at least get credit for honesty, but always trying your damnedest to be good enough, and ending up with a mountain of misery on your back because you knew you were not, never would be good enough. Meanwhile, I knew the Christian doctrine of grace, knew it with full-headed Calvinistic orthodoxy. But I did not live it inside my feelings, not enough to steer me clear of hideous depressions, all of them sealing me inside a room whose walls had one message scrawled all over them, "You are not worthy, you are not worthy," and the walls sometimes pressed, squeezed, crowded me close to despair.

As I walked in that small space, back and forth, from the living room sofa to the dining room table, bent low at the hips, looking, I suppose, like an arthritic Ichabod Crane, sadness seizing my whole being, I began to feel as if all those human hands, all their stroking, all their approving patting, all were taken away from me. Now I not only felt like a hypocrite for wanting them too much, I felt deserted by them when I needed them; and I began to panic. It was as if mother were saying: "I can never give you my approval after all, never, not ever; you are not, never will be good enough for me to love you." It was as if my closest friends, the ones I needed most, were saying, "Sorry, we cannot reach you there. We cannot help you." And all the other people in my life joined the chorus: "We cannot help you." All the hands I needed were drawn away. None stayed to hold me.

They left me alone. But without them, I knew I would fall. And I did fall, down, down, down, into a nothingness; into a void, an abyss, a mocking empty hole of unworthiness and helplessness.

I had never known such lonely pain, never such fear, never such helplessness, never such despair. I was lost, utterly lost. I felt a life of pious trying going down the drain, a life of half-baked belief in grace exposed as futile. I was sunk. I screamed for help, and none could come. I was making my bed in hell.

I lay down in my spiritual waste. But I did not sink! When I flopped into nothingness I fell into God. The old Hebrew lyricist was right, you can make your bed in hell and find your rest in God's hands. It is not a terrible thing to fall into the hands of the living God. No matter what Jonathan Edwards said. His hands are pierced with nails from

Christ's cross; his hands are the strength of his love, the power to hold us and keep us from falling into a hell without God.

I discovered, all by myself, in touch only with my final outpost of feeling, that I could be left, deserted, alone, all my scaffolds knocked down, all the stanchions beneath me pulled away, my buttresses fallen, I could be stripped of human hands, and I could survive. In my deepest heart I survived, stood up, stayed whole, held by nothing at all except the grace of a loving God.

I was in the hands of God.

I could live by grace.

I could lose all human support and not fall down.

I was held, and would not be dropped. I was supported, and would not sink. I was held together, and would not fall apart. I was accepted, and could not be rejected. I was loved, and would never be despised. I was in hell, and God was there for me. I knew then he would be in all my mini-hells, and my mini-heavens too.

I knelt in front of the mousy blue sofa in the living room, to thank God for holding me up. I thanked him that, with him, I did not need to be good enough. I could flourish without mother's approval. I could survive without the comfort sucked from silken stroking by significant people. I thanked him that he was there, to accept me "without one plea but that thy blood was shed for me," and to keep me in one piece above the pit of despair. I felt love, so I knew I felt God. Or was it the other way around? Did I feel God and so knew I felt love? I can never keep the order straight. No matter. I felt it was all right with me when I felt everything was all wrong.

What is it like to feel God in hell? I have not cultivated the mystic's knack for metaphors to match an experience of God. To tell the truth, I felt no sweet passion seducing me into the embrace of Jesus. I did not feel like a drop of human water swallowed into an ocean of divinity. I heard no divine flute piping me into lyrical ecstasy. I was not even flooded by heavenly sunshine. What I felt was the sober, ultimate relief of knowing that I could face the worst and not be destroyed, that I could live without mother's pat on my head, and that I could be myself and, in some Christian sense, not give a damn, when the chips are down, whether mother or anyone else approves of me or not. Because I knew that I was held together by God's unconditional Christ-won love. I knew it could be all right with me when everything else was kaput.

If no human hand ever again pounded my shoulder to tell me I was one of the gang, I could survive.

If no human hand ever grabbed mine to tell me I had a friend, I could survive.

If no hand ever deftly brushed my lips to tell me I was cherished, I could survive.

If no loving hand rested on my forehead when I died, I could survive.

If no churchly hand were stretched over my dead body to give me a parting benediction, I could survive.

I can survive the minor hell of having no human hand to help me because I am held in hell by the hand of God. What I felt, then, was not sweetness so much as strength. There is a courage that comes from being held by God in hell, a courage to be what you are, knowing that what you are is a person who can never be anywhere without being with a God who holds you up. Yes, what I felt was more like courage than like piety.

All of it is parable, I know. I know my hell on Fox Island was the hell of my inner feelings of lostness. I know the hands of God were the grace of God keeping me from feeling condemned. What I discovered in feeling was what I have known in intellect for years, that we are held together in our being, and loved in our sinfulness, by a God whose power and grace are everywhere, even in our hells. The difference is that, here, I actually *felt him* holding me, and I knew as I felt that he would never let me go.

By grace! I was accepted, no strings, as the ridiculously ambiguous person I am, accepted without qualification, by God. By faith! I felt God without a fleck of hard evidence that it was really he whom I felt holding me, without any sure guarantee that he would not draw back sometime and leave me when the mood was on him. By his grace and my faith, I felt the living God, and knew at the heart of the matter it was all right. I came through the afternoon the way St. Paul got through Romans 7 with all its "who shall deliver me?" sort of mini-hell, when he said: "I am dead sure that neither death or life . . . can ever come between us and the love of God that came to us in Jesus Christ our Lord."

Can I be sure you understand? I am talking about an experience of feeling, like the feeling you have when somebody you love is with you in the darkness of a strange place. I am not talking about a belief that God will take care of you. For instance, take the belief that God has a plan for our lives, and that he planned our voyage through hell for a purpose. Maybe he did plan it all; I will not deny it. But believing that God planned it is not the same as feeling God in it. Even if I do believe that he planned it all back there, behind time's door, I may not *experience him,* now, in my hell. What I experienced, and hope you have too, is God himself, here *in* my mini-hell.

Another thing I am not saying is that something good will happen to you after you get *out* of your private hell, a sweet twist of loving providence, a divine wind to blow away pain, an air-lift from Sheol. Miracles are nice, I am sure, though they do not happen much to me. But what I am trying to say is that God will be there *in* your hell, not afterward, but in it, contrary to rumor and against all the odds, in hell with you, putting his love beneath you and holding you up in the time of your God-forsakenness.

Maybe, just to make sure, I should also say that feeling God in our private hells is not the same as finding an answer to the problem of suffering. Some people have to suffer much more than others; innocent children are beaten by adults and starved by nature. The unfairness and the horror of much suffering is the most compelling reason sensitive skeptics have ever had for not believing in God. How can a good God, able to do whatever he wills, allow such enormous suffering inside his world? I do not know the answer. I do not know how nine thousand Jewish people could be fed into the Auschwitz gas ovens every day, while God was watching and weeping in heaven. I do not have a satisfying theory of what he was doing in Auschwitz. I *believe* he was keeping to the rules of the divine-human game; that having created free agents he would let them be free, even to do the most horrible things we can imagine.

Anyway, my experience up at Fox Island was not the answer to the problem of Auschwitz or other monstrous horrors. It was an answer to the infinitely smaller question of how I could survive when no people were able to succor me. I can only witness to the reality of God's presence for me, in my mini-hell, the hell where I made my own bed. I have not been in Auschwitz. I have only been in my own hell, and I know God was there for me. I only hope that many whose bed was made for them in the Auschwitz hell found him even there, to hold them and keep them from falling forever.

It does not come easy for me to press the integrity of religious feelings. Everything in my lifestyle, my character, my tradition tells me not to trust my feelings. Especially religious feelings. Feelings will play you false. They will tempt you to want good feelings more than you want truth about the living God. I know every sound reason there is why you should trust your head instead of your heart. But I also know that my feelings did not play me false; I know that what I felt was not my lower stomach, I know it was God.

When it comes to God, in fact, our minds are as tricky as our feelings. I know that my brains have often made a fool out of me with God. Early on, I conned myself into supposing that, if I had a clear head focused on a clear doctrine of divine grace, I would actually be experiencing grace. What a cock-

eyed religious idiot I was. Mind you, I would n̲...
have admitted that I believed theology was a wor̲...
able substitute for experience; I just acted the fantasy out.

I am not the only idiot with an inclination for
confusing clear thinking about reality with experiencing reality. I have known Christians who
thought they must be specially good folk because
they alone taught that all of us are corrupted by
original sin. And I have thought that I could *be* all
right if I only had a well-balanced *doctrine* of all
rightness. So if you, like the rest of us religious
elitists, are more head than heart, and if you are a
bit of an intellectual snob, as I am, I hope you will at
least give the devil his due and admit that he can
seduce your brain as easily as he can beguile your
feelings.

I must admit that the trip from head down to
heart, from thinking to feeling, is pain all the way.
We pay a fairly steep price for feeling God in hell. I
think we feel his presence most profoundly if we
have felt his absence; we feel him nearest after we
have been sure he must be somewhere else. Sometimes you need to feel that you are lost, sinking,
desolate, alone, if you want to feel for sure that God
is there, hands holding you even in your mini-hell.

I am at the end of my story. I wanted to tell you
that one way to discover how it can be all right with
us when everything is wrong is to fall into God
when you are sinking into hell, your own hell,
however its special flames may sear you. Being held
by God is a gift of grace. You cannot press buttons,
turn keys, manipulate people, say magic words, to
get God in place. But he is there, even when you

ere when you "know" for sure he is
you need to do is let yourself sink into
hen all your supports have been ripped
all hands have stopped stroking you,
u feel is the horror of neglect, he is
there, underneath, and will never let you fall.

I do not recommend hell, not even a mini-hell, to
anyone. Hell, anyone's hell, hurts too much. So if
you can feel God in your mini-heavens of all-rightness, be content. But there is a chance that you may
have to make your bed in hell, sometime, and you
may feel as if you had fallen there before your time,
alone, helpless, everything gone wrong at the core,
instant God-forsakenness. If you do, or when you
do, you may, as I did, feel God closer to you than
when everything was heavenly. God is there, ahead
of time, before you get there, waiting, hands open,
to hold you when you are sure you are sinking. You
will feel his presence, feel his strength, feel the
courage that comes from his support, if you just let
him hold you. And when you do feel him, you will
know that it will be all right with you, at that
moment, later, or any time. Do not ask me how you
can be sure. I, for one, have no guarantee that it will
happen to you. But I know it can. You will know it
too, when you feel yourself falling out of reach of
the human hands you need, falling away from them
and landing in God's hands. You will feel, at bottom, that no one but God himself is holding you and
you will know that, in spite of everything, it all is
right with you.

12. Everything Is Going to Be All Right!

◆§ THE GIFT OF HOPE §◆

We wait for new heavens and a new earth in which righteousness dwells. And hope does not disappoint us.

2 Pet. 3:13; Rom. 5:5, RSV

I bought a brand new date book yesterday, the kind I use every year, spiral-bound, black imitation leather covers wrapped around pages and pages of blank squares. Each square has a number to tell me which day of the month I am in at the moment. Each square is a frame for one episode of my life. Before I am through with the book, I will fill the squares with classes I will teach, people I will eat lunch with, and everlasting committee meetings I will sit through. And these are only the things I cannot afford to forget; I fill the squares, too, with things I do not write down for me to remember, thousands of cups of coffee, some lovemaking, some praying, and, I hope, gestures of help to my neighbors. Whatever I do, it has to fit inside one of those squares on my date book.

I live one square at a time. The four lines that make the square are the walls of time that organize my life. Everything I do has to fit into one square; I cannot straddle the lines.

Each square has an invisible door that leads to the next square. At a silent stroke, the door opens and I am pulled through it as if by a magnet, sucked into the next square in the line. There I will again fill the time frame that seals me, fill it with my busyness, just as I did the square before. As I get older, the squares seem to get smaller.

One day, I will walk into a square that has no door. There will be no mysterious opening, and no walking into an adjoining square. One of the squares will be terminal. I do not know which square it will be.

A life insurance person can roughly guess the squares I may expect before I get to the last one. How many do I have left? Suppose I have exactly 1,029 squares left. What difference would it make to me now as I fill up *this* square, the only one that holds me today? The difference depends, not so much on how many squares are left, but on what really is going to happen to me when I get to that final square.

Two things can happen. Which of the two does happen tells pretty much what life is and what our world is all about. So we ought to face the two possibilities with utter honesty. This is no time for make-believe. The first possibility is that when I walk into the last square, the one with no door, I will be suffocated inside of it. The walls of the square may close in on me, as it were, to choke me. All my yesterdays may have only vomited me into this dark room with no exit; I may have strutted my petty pace through each day only to be seduced into this blank square that silences my sounds forever. I have pretended in all those squares to be somebody special; now I may share my bed with dead rats. This could be what happens to me 1,029 squares from now. And if it happens to me, it likely happens to everybody, whenever he slides into the final square of his datebook.

The second possibility is that when I walk into the last square, I will discover that the reason it has no door is that it has no walls for a door to fit into. The four unmovable lines that sealed me inside all my other frames are erased. The last day of my life turns out to be the beginning of life in new dimensions, free somehow, because the walls of regulated time have fallen away. The last square is not death; it is a new dimension of life.

The Christian gospel comes down to a promise that the second possibility is the real one; our last square is an introduction into a new expansive world of perfect peace and total justice. When we believe the promise, we have what is called the Christian hope. We may as well be very candid: Christian hope is fixed on the last square of our date book. Hope bets that the last square is not that closed closet commonly called a coffin, but a front door into a new world where everything is right, right in all dimensions.

There will be an intermission, of course, between my arrival at my own private last square and the arrival of the new world. But I will not feel as if I need to wait for it to come. In fact, when I find myself in the new earth, I will feel as if I got there at the moment I left the last square of my calendar. It may be light years away, but in the new dimension it will seem like tomorrow.

I said it will be a new world. But it will be new the way an old, ramshackled, broken-down house is new after it has been worked over from top to bottom, outside and inside, by an architect with a clear eye for renewing a misused structure whose foundations are still sound. Everything is new compared with the dilapidated hulk that the house had become. But it is still the same old house that it was when its very first people moved in. Totally new; fundamentally the same. So it is with the new earth we hope for.

The new earth is this old world. We will recognize its oceans and rivers, green places, dry places, peaks and valleys, animals and people who live together. It will be the same earth that the Creator made and loved, the garden he planned for his children, the kingdom he refused to surrender to the enemy. So what is new about it?

What is new about it, mostly, is the way people live together and with God. Human beings for the first time will always be fair to each other, to begin with; and the arrangements we make for our lives together—the institutions and structures—will support the justice the Bible demanded early on. St. Peter says that we look for a new earth where everything is right. The Bible calls it righteousness; biblical righteousness is pretty much what we mean when we wish everything were all right with our world.

Rightness begins with justice, with people getting

what they have coming to them. But it includes much more. Everything is right, not just in a legal sense that people all get what is due them. Life is right because people care about each other, love each other, and never let each other down.

When we hope for a world where everything is right we hope for still more; we hope for what the Bible calls *Shalom,* a word we translate as peace, only it means much more than what we usually call peace. Peace, in the new world, is a life charged with joy, health, and love. When you read in the book of Revelation (21:4) that God will "wipe away every tear from their eyes, and death shall be no more, neither shall there be mourning nor crying nor pain anymore," you get at least a negative hint of what the Bible means by peace. Anyway, when the walls of that last square in our calendar dissolve, they free us to live in this very new world of magnificent rightness.

There is a lot of silly talk in some Christian circles these days about the "end of the world," as if Christians are supposed to look forward to a huge holocaust in which God destroys his own creation. What absolute rubbish! One man has even written a best-seller about "the *late* great planet earth." A piece of contemptible silliness that insults the planet's Creator! He loves our world and he has no plans to preside over its demise. His plan is to make it all right again. "Late planet"? Nonsense! The very notion is probably the sickest heresy ever to corrupt the Christian hope.

The nightmare of an "end of the world" makes it very hard for people to hope for God's future. I asked a group of Christian people once if they wanted to go to heaven when they died. As best I remember, they all raised their hands. Then I asked if they would like to go today, if given the chance, now, before the sun sets. A couple of people raised their hands, slowly, sneaking a look around to see if they were alone, and they were. Most people wanted to put heaven off for a while; a rain check, if you please, and why not—if going to heaven means you never set foot on earth again?

Then I asked if they would like to see the world we live in set straight on its hinges, once and for all, tomorrow. There would be no common colds and no uncommon cancers. Everyone would have his day; there would be no second class citizens. Prisoners and slaves would be free; hungry people would have plenty; no one would lift a finger to harm another; and we would all be at peace with everyone, especially with ourselves. Our nationalist swords would be smithed into international plows, and we would all have peace at last. A show of hands? A frenzy of hand lifting. And I said: if a new world tomorrow is what you really want, you want to go to heaven. For heaven is nothing more than this earth made new. What else would a good Creator plan for his earthly creatures?

The Christian hope has eyes on this world, for this is the world God made, the world to which he sent his Son, not to condemn it, but to save it (John 3:17). God will be its magnetic center. Jesus will be its Lord. And all who live in it will perfectly praise its Maker and Redeemer.

For some people, seeing God and seeing Jesus is everything good about heaven:

Father of Jesus, Love Divine
What rapture it will be,
Prostrate before Thy throne to lie,
And gaze and gaze on thee.

Personally, I need a little more. I think God is pleased when we enjoy his earth while we enjoy him. He knows that some of us need more than an undiluted version of his beauty; we need each other's beauty, too. So, while God is the heart, he does not ask to be the whole. I am thankful to him for letting us find our joy in each other as well as in him. We may gaze on him Sundays; weekdays he will let us play and work with our brothers and sisters of the human family. And heaven will be as fine on Monday as it is on Sunday.

We have been talking about what it is we hope for. Now I want to shift our focus, and talk about what we do when we hope. The word "hope" points both ways—ahead to what we hope for and inward to our own experience of hoping. I'm going to talk now of our experience. Forget for now about the future. Get hold of yourself; you say you have hope, that you really do hope that everything will be all right. Try now to think of what it is like to hope, to do what we do when we hope for something, anything at all.

It seems to me that three things are going on in us whenever we hope for something. The first is desire; we want what we hope for. The second is belief; we believe that what we hope for is possible. The third is doubt; we fear that what we hope for may not happen. Suppose I expand on these just a bit.

Hoping is desiring; we want something we do not yet have. Merely believing that certain things are going to happen in the future is not the same as hoping that they will happen. When I was a boy, I was warned that Jesus might come at any minute; but I wanted him to wait, at least long enough for the Detroit Tigers to win the World Series. I believed, in a way, but I did not hope for his coming. Only when I really wanted Jesus to come did I begin to hope he would.

Hoping is also believing; we believe that what we want in the future *may* actually happen. Hope builds on possibilities. If I know for sure that I cannot be cured, I give up hoping for a cure. If I know for sure that I shall be cured, I do not need to hope. I hope only as long as I believe that what I want is possible, even though it is not inevitable.

When we hope we also doubt; we cannot help doubting because we cannot be sure. Doubt is the third dimension of hoping. If it is possible for my team to win, it is also possible for it to lose. If it is possible that we may find a cure for cancer, it is also possible that we will not find one. Human hope is always a risk. With a lot of good luck we may feed the hungry people of the world out of our resources; with some bad luck, we could set off nuclear disaster for everyone. So we place our bets, and we hope, believing and doubting at the same time. This is human hoping.

So much for what we do when we hope for things in general. Now I want to ask what we do in our *Christian* hoping that is different from ordinary hoping. I think the difference settles on the third dimension: doubt. Christian hoping is not believing in the possible; it is a conviction about what is sure. Christian hoping is a gift of certainty that what God promises he will most assuredly give. This is why St. Paul calls it a "hope that never disappoints" (Rom. 5:5). It is why the writer of Hebrews (6:9) calls Christian hope a "sure and steadfast anchor for the soul." The doubt factor is extracted from human hoping; possibility becomes certainty.

For this reason, Christian hoping comes only as a gift of grace. We do not hope in a Christian style because we are smart enough to bet on a winner. Our hope is not based on a shrewd reading between the lines of the *New York Times*. In fact, if we are honest about it, what we hope for really seems quite ridiculously impossible. Common sense could tell us that Christian hoping is a wild card bet on what can never come to pass.

The tough students of history insist that nothing will ever change radically for the better. There is no golden age in our past to prove for sure that a "new earth where everything is all right" is a feasible alternative to our battered globe. There is a dark age to tell us for sure that human beings are capable of every evil the mind can conceive. We have Auschwitz in our record. We have no City of God. We have unending rows of innocent persons herded into gas chambers every day. We have no model in history of people living together in mutual respect and universal love. No, if Christian hoping is "feeling absolutely sure," it runs smack against the brutalities of the race's experience with reality.

Surely there must be an insider's tip, some signal from an unimpeachable, if unnamed, source, some absolutely undeniable leak from high places, to

171

make us so sure. No; what we have is a promise. And a power to *hear* the promise, believe it, and live by it. Just a promise? Yes, just a promise. We wait, says the apostle, we wait for a new earth *according to his promise* (2 Pet. 3:13). What a promise! As wide as all earth, total, the ultimate signal of all-rightness.

The promise always had to do with a new and better world, a world of peace and joy to rise from the rubble of our wars and sadness. "For behold I create new heavens and a new earth" (Is. 65:1). Swords beaten into plows; lions sleeping alongside of lambs; the poor given justice; the weak raised to positions of strength; and all peoples enjoying the *Shalom* of God. This was the promise that percolated into the consciousness of the ancient folk who otherwise had no hope at all.

Later, the promise came to us as a person whose whole existence was a way of saying, "There is a better world coming." A little Jewish girl, his mother-to-be, stunned by her pregnancy, was inspired to sing of a day when he had "filled the hungry with good things, and sent the rich away empty" (Luke 2:53). While a baby was born in poverty, the angels sang that he would bring peace to the whole world. He grew up, doing strange and wonderful things that signaled the power of all-rightness with him: a village harlot becomes a loving woman, a man crippled all his life suddenly jumps on his two feet, a blind man sees trees and children, people chained to their sense of guilt are set free, and here and there a dead man walks out of a tomb. He said that he came to preach liberty to captives and freedom to the oppressed, and his miracles were hints that the promise was going to come true over all the earth.

The baby grew up and became a threat to established powers. So they hanged him on a cross and let him die. But God raised him up again, and in doing so put flesh and blood on the promise of a new earth to come. Many people feel the spirit of this risen man in their own spirits; when they do, they believe the promise and are certain that it is true. Hope is their gift. And they live by it as they move too fast from small square to small square on their way to the last one, the one that frightens people so much.

The gift of hope is, frankly, fixed on the final square on our calendar; and only hope can take away the dread of that last square. All the hopes we have for better times in between are human hopes, and human hoping always invites human doubting to join it. We can be absolutely sure only that everything is going to be all right *in the end*.

The vision of the last square on our date books, however, sheds its light on all the squares in between. We live in hope and hope lights up our lives. We see each square differently because we see that last one as the entrée to a new earth. In a way, I know it is all right with me, now, when everything may be wrong, *because* I hope that everything is going to be all right for all of us in God's new earth of the future.

I hope, with human hope, that my friend's retarded child will become an intelligent adult; but I doubt that she will. I hope, with Christian hope, that her present handicap is a brief prelude to real life as a person of limitless creative intelligence. My human hope for her cure within the squares of her calendar is slim; but I have great hopes for her, and my hopes for her make her as precious on this earth as any creative genius.

I hope, with human hope, that my community will be a fair place for people to live, a place where people help each other, care for each other, and where all people have both enough to eat and someone to love them. But I doubt that I will ever find such a perfect community. I hope, with Christian hope, that we will all love each other with a love that finds its highest pleasure when other people have what is rightly theirs, capped with inexpressible joys. And my sure hope for a community of perfect love and perfect justice makes my present human family worth saving and healing.

The gift of hope makes every person, as well as the whole family of humanity, very valuable; the vision of future rightness sends back a stamp of rightness into the present. It also makes life a little more playful. What we cannot do in a million calendar squares, God will do in his own time. So the new world will not be lost if we play a little on our way. Besides, when we play we are modeling life in heaven. "Old men and old women shall again sit in the streets of Jerusalem, each with staff in hand for every age. And the city shall be full of boys and girls playing in the streets" (Zech. 8:4, 5). What it comes to is this: Christian hope makes good work meaningful, but it tells us that we cannot live by work alone. Let the squares on our calendars be meadows for dancing.

Many people live without Christian hope. Some of them drink and drug themselves so that they can forget the tedium of their squares lining up, the same, one after another. Others fill their allotted squares with shopping and consuming. Still others work their squares away and become very rich, and neurotic, and end up wondering about the meaning of the squares. After all, what do all the date books come to anyway, all those squares that millions upon millions of people fill with their fretting and fuming? Could anthropologist Ernest Becker be right? "The soberest conclusion that we could make about what has been taking place on the planet for about three billion years is that it is being turned into a vast pit of fertilizer."* This is sweet human hope turned to sour doubt.

The only real answer to soured human hope is certain Christian hope. I believe that Becker is wrong, and I will know it by experience when I walk into the last square on my life's agenda. For there I will discover that this earth has become the Kingdom of my Lord Jesus Christ, and that everything good and noble and decent that human beings have known during their walk through the squares will flourish there, transformed, in the life to come, and that the earth will be the splendid place of justice and of love through the power of God's Spirit, to the glory of our great Creator and Redeemer. There, at last, all will be right with us, and everything else will be all right too.

---

*Ernest Becker, *The Denial of Death* (New York: The Free Press, 1973), p. 283.

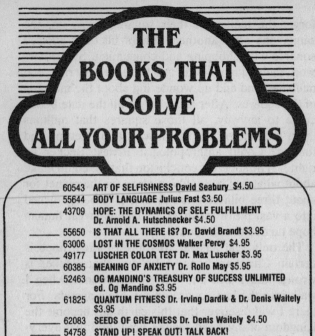

THE BOOKS THAT SOLVE ALL YOUR PROBLEMS

_____	60543	ART OF SELFISHNESS David Seabury $4.50
_____	55644	BODY LANGUAGE Julius Fast $3.50
_____	43709	HOPE: THE DYNAMICS OF SELF FULFILLMENT Dr. Arnold A. Hutschnecker $4.50
_____	55650	IS THAT ALL THERE IS? Dr. David Brandt $3.95
_____	63006	LOST IN THE COSMOS Walker Percy $4.95
_____	49177	LUSCHER COLOR TEST Dr. Max Luscher $3.95
_____	60385	MEANING OF ANXIETY Dr. Rollo May $5.95
_____	52463	OG MANDINO'S TREASURY OF SUCCESS UNLIMITED ed. Og Mandino $3.95
_____	61825	QUANTUM FITNESS Dr. Irving Dardik & Dr. Denis Waitely $3.95
_____	62083	SEEDS OF GREATNESS Dr. Denis Waitely $4.50
_____	54758	STAND UP! SPEAK OUT! TALK BACK! The Key to Self-Assertive Therapy. Robert E. Alberti & Michael Emmons $3.50
_____	62224	SUCCESS THROUGH A POSITIVE MENTAL ATTITUDE Napoleon Hill & W.C. Stone $4.50
_____	46424	THE OWNER'S MANUAL FOR YOUR LIFE Stewart Emery $3.50
_____	54757	THE SKY'S THE LIMIT Dr. Wayne Dyer $4.50
_____	52462	THE SUCCESS SYSTEM THAT NEVER FAILS W. Clement Stone $3.95
_____	55768	UP FROM DEPRESSION Leonard Cammer, M.D. $3.95
_____	60405	TOO YOUNG TO DIE Francine Klagsbrun $3.50

POCKET BOOKS, Department PPA
1230 Avenue of the Americas, New York, N.Y. 10020

Please send me the books I have checked above. I am enclosing $_____
(please add 75¢ to cover postage and handling, N.Y.S. and N.Y.C. residents please
add appropriate sales tax). Send check or money order—no cash or C.O.D.s please.
Allow six weeks for delivery. For purchases over $10.00, you may use VISA: card
number, expiration date and customer signature must be included.

NAME_____

ADDRESS_____

CITY_____STATE/ZIP_____

943